Anonymous

Juvenile Gems of Song and Story

Anonymous

Juvenile Gems of Song and Story

ISBN/EAN: 9783337375317

Printed in Europe, USA, Canada, Australia, Japan

Cover: Foto ©Thomas Meinert / pixelio.de

More available books at **www.hansebooks.com**

JUVENILE GEMS

OF

SONG AND STORY.

NEW YORK:
JOHN B. ALDEN, PUBLISHER.
1886.

CONTENTS.

	PAGE.
Good Night and Good Morning. By Lord Houghton	9
April Voices. By Amelia Daley Alden	10
The Builders. By Henry W. Longfellow	12
Little Boy Blue. By Abby Sage Richardson	13
The Story of the Wind. By Amanda T. Jones	14
Our Mother's Sampler. By Susan Teall Perry	15
Little Florence. By Ellen Tracy Alden	17
Prayers of the Children. By Frances S. Osgood	21
Bed-Time. By Josephine Pollard	22
The Might of Truth. By Alice Cary	23
The Beautiful Hand. By Clara Doty Bates	24
Judge Not. By Adelaide Anne Proctor	25
Song of Marion's Men. By William Cullen Bryant	26
The Relief of Lucknow. By Robert Lowell	28
Perseverance. By R. S. S. Andros	30
The Heritage. By James Russell Lowell	33
The Nurse's Song. By Susan Coolidge	34
Apple Blossoms. By Mary A. P. Stansbury	36
Baby-Land. By George Cooper	38
A Centennial Tea-Pot. By Ellen Tracy Alden	39
Words. By Adelaide Anne Proctor	42
Little Harry and the New Moon. By Helen E. Brown	43
The Story of Mother Becker. By Amanda T. Jones	46
Christ and the Little Ones. By Julia Gill	49
Paul Revere's Ride. By Henry W. Longfellow	50
The Old Continentals. By Guy Humphrey McMaster	54
Wait. By Ward Steele	56
King Canute. By William Makepeace Thackeray	57
A Little Philosopher. By Margaret E. Sangster	61
Arachne. By Dora Read Goodale	62
The Voice of the Grass. By Sarah Roberts	63
The Dandelions. By Amelia D. Alden	64
Grandmother's Story of Bunker Hill Battle. By Oliver Wendell Holmes	65
The Inchcape Rock. By Robert Southey	74
The Humble-Bee. By Ralph Waldo Emerson	76
Bruce and the Spider. By Bernard Barton	78
To a Waterfowl. By William Cullen Bryant	79
Baby's Skies. By M. C. Bartlett	80
Who Stole the Bird's Nest. By Mrs. L. M. Child	81
The Cat's Dinner-Time. By Elizabeth Akers Allen	83

CONTENTS.

	PAGE
To Mother Fairie. By Alice Cary	84
The Gladness of Nature. By William Cullen Bryant	85
Suppose! By Phœbe Cary	86
An Incident of the Fire at Hamburg. By James Russell Lowell	87
Landing of the Pilgrim Fathers. By Felicia Hemans	90
To the Lady-Bird. By Mrs. Southey	91
The Season that is Coming. By Mrs. M. F. Butts	92
Queen Mabel. By Ellen Tracy Alden	93
They Didn't Think. By Phœbe Cary	99
A Mystery. By Reaf Coral	101
The Secret. By Mrs. F. L. Ballard	102
The Common Question. By John Greenleaf Whittier	103
Fable. By Ralph Waldo Emerson	104
Baby. By George MacDonald	105
Robert of Lincoln. By William Cullen Bryant	106
Small Beginnings. By Charles Mackay	108
A Psalm of Life. By Henry W. Longfellow	109
The Fairy Wedding. By Amelia Daley Alden	110
High-Tide on the Cost of Lincolnshire. By Jean Ingelow	112
Buttercups and Daisies. By Mary Howitt	117
Song of the Brook. By Alfred Tennyson	119
Wild Geese. By Celia Thaxter	120
The Tradespeople. By Julius Sturm	121
Take Care. By Alice Cary	122
Sir Patrick Spens. *An Old Ballad*	123
The Destruction of Sennacherib. By Byron	126
The Better Land. By Felicia Hemans	128
The King Speaks. By Will H. Veith	129
Casabianca. By Felicia Hemans	130
Giant and Dwarf. By William Allen Butler	131
Baby Bye. By Theodore Tilton	133
Katy. By Ellen Tracy Alden	136
The Motherless Turkeys. By Marian Douglass	137
Tiny Tokens. By Frances Ridley Havergal	139
The Song of Steam. By G. W. Cutter	140
The Last Hymn. By Marianne Farmingham	142
Dutiful Jem. By Jane Taylor	144
The Brown Thrush. By Lucy Larcom	146
Seven Times One. By Jean Ingelow	147
The Heavenly Friend. By Anna Shipton	148
The Signs of the Season. By M. E. N. Hathaway	150
The First Tangle. By Anna F. Burnham	151
A Builder's Lesson. By John Boyle O'Reilly	152
The Fairy Isle. By Louise V. Boyd	153
The Arab's Farewell to His Steed. By Mrs. Norton	156
The Battle of Blenheim. By Robert Southey	159
Dream of the Golden Age. By Persie Vere	161
Grandma's Corner. By Augusta Moore	163

CONTENTS.

	PAGE.
The Little Yellow Bee. By Mary L. Bolles Branch	164
Winsome Maggie. By Ellen Tracy Alden	166
"Somebody's Mother." *Home Journal*	168
Woodman Spare That Tree. By Geo. P. Morris	169
Be Honest and True	170
One Saturday. By Marion Douglass	171
The Sea. By Barry Cornwall	173
The Brown Thrush. By Lucy Larcom	174
The Little Cavalier. By Geo. Cooper	175
The Wind Blows. By Dora Read Goodale	176
A Danish Legend. By Caroline M. Hewins	177
The Pied Piper of Hamelin. By Robert Browning	179
The Spider and the Fly. By Mary Howitt	185
The Wise Fairy. By Alice Cary	188
The Death of the Flowers. By William Cullen Bryant	189
The Secret of a Happy Day By Frances Ridley Havergal	191
The Color-Bearer. By J. T. Trowbridge	193
Day-Dreams. By Annie M. Libby	195
The Brook that Ran Into the Sea. By Lucy Larcom	196
Work. By Mary N. Prescott	198
Before Snow Time. By James Berry Bensel	199
Light For All. *S. S. Advocate.*	200
A Visit from St. Nicholas. By Clement C. Moore	201
A Dinner and a Kiss	203
The Angel's Blessing By Amelia Daley Alden	204
The Angel's Song. By Edmund H. Sears	205
A Christmas Carol. By Mrs. J. K. Hervey	206
Christmas. By Margaret Sidney	209
Little By Little. *Youth's Companion*	211
Old Christmas. By Mary Howitt	212
An Old Legend. By Rose Terry	214
The Three Kings. By H. W. Longfellow	216
Christmas Time. By Sir Walter Scott	218
The Christmas Story. By Nahum Tate	220
Jacky's Sock and Jennie's Stocking. By Helen Stannard	221
Brightest and Best. By Reginald Heber	223
Contentment. By Frances S. Osgood,	224

JUVENILE GEMS
OF
SONG AND STORY.

GOOD-NIGHT AND GOOD-MORNING.

A FAIR little girl
Sat under a tree,
Sewing as long as
Her eyes could see;
She smoothed her work,
And folded it right,
And said, " Dear work,
Good-night, good-night."

Such a number of rooks
Went over her head,
Crying, " Caw, caw,"
On their way to bed,
She said, as she watched
Their curious flight,
" Little black things,
Good-night, good-night."

The horses neighed,
And the oxen lowed,
And the sheep's " bleat, bleat "
Came over the road,
All seeming to say,
With a quiet delight,
" Good little girl,
Good-night, good-night."

She did not say
To the sun " Good-night,"
Though she saw him there
Like a ball of light;
For she knew he had
God's time to keep
All over the world,
And never could sleep.

The tall, pink fox-glove
Bowed her head;
The violets curtsied
And went to bed;
And good little Lucy
Tied up her hair,
And said, on her knees,
Her favorite prayer.

And while on her pillow
She softly lay,
She heard nothing more
Till again it was day.
And all things said
To the beautiful sun,
" Good-morning, good-morning;
Our work has begun."
Lord Houghton.

APRIL VOICES.

WHEN winter snows have melted,
    And in April's sunny track
The sparrow, and the phebe-bird,
    And blue-bird venture back;

When the days are growing longer,
    And the buds begin to swell,
And, noiselessly, the sun unlocks
    Each blossom's winter cell;

Then listen at some hillside ;
　Put your ear against the earth ;
And you may hear a murmuring—
　A faint sweet sound of mirth,

As if from some far country
　The wandering wind should bring
A murmur of the melody
　That tuneful joy-bells ring,

And gush of childish laughter,
　Across the meadows blown,
Should mingle with the chiming,
　In a happy undertone.

But 'tis not distant chiming,
　Nor sound of childish glee,
That gushes from the hillside's heart,
　As sweet as sweet can be.

It comes from souls of blossoms,
　That long have waiting lain,
For April suns to call them forth
　To outward life again.

The violet is calling
　To the bloodroot frail and fair ;
The dandelion laughs aloud
　At thought of sun and air ;

And longs to throw his blossoms,
　Like stars, upon the grass,
And feel the children's little feet
　Among them lightly pass.

The cowslip and the daisy,
　The clovers, red and white,
The bluebell and the buttercup,
　Are longing for the light.

And all their voices blending,
　Ring out so sweet and clear,
That he who listens earnestly
　The merry tones may hear.
　　　　　　Amelia Daley Alden.

THE BUILDERS.

ALL are architects of Fate,
   Working in these walls of Time;
Some with massive deeds and great,
   Some with ornaments of rhyme.

Nothing useless is or low;
   Each thing in its place is best;
And what seems but idle show
   Strengthens and supports the rest.

For the structure that we raise
   Time is with materials filled;
Our to-days and yesterdays
   Are the blocks with which we build.

Truly shape and fashion these,
   Leave no yawning gaps between;
Think not, because no man sees,
   Such things will remain unseen.

In the elder days of Art,
   Builders wrought with greatest care
Each minute and unseen part;
   For the gods see everywhere.

Let us do our work as well,
   Both the unseen and the seen;
Make the house where gods may dwell,
   Beautiful, entire and clean.

Else our lives are incomplete,
   Standing in these walls of Time,
Broken stairways, where the feet
   Stumble as they seek to climb.

Build to-day, then, strong and sure,
   With a firm and ample base;
And ascending and secure
   Shall to-morrow find its place.

Thus alone can we attain
To those turrets, where the eye
Sees the world as one vast plain,
And one boundless reach of sky.
Henry W. Longfellow.

LITTLE BOY BLUE.

UNDER the hay-stack little Boy Blue
   Sleeps with his head on his arm,
While voices of men and voices of maids
   Are calling him over the farm.

Sheep in the meadows are running wild,
   Where poisonous herbage grows ;
Leaving white tufts of downy fleece
   On the thorns of the sweet wild-rose.

Out in the fields where the silken corn
   Its plumed head nods and bows,
Where golden pumpkins ripen below,
   Trample the white-faced cows.

But no loud blast on the shining horn
   Calls back the straying sheep ;
And the cows may wander in hay or corn,
   While their keeper lies asleep.

His roguish eyes are tightly shut,
   His dimples are all at rest ;
The chubby hand, tucked under his head,
   By one rosy cheek is pressed.

Waken him ? No. Let down the bars,
   And gather the truant sheep ;
Open the barnyard and drive in the cows,
   But let the little boy sleep.

For year after year we can shear the fleece,
   And corn can always be sown ;
But the sleep that visits little Boy Blue
   Will not come when the years have flown.
Abby Sage Richardson.

THE STORY OF THE WIND.

THE wind came over the hills one day,
  Singing a charming tune,
As light and low as the sleepy lay
  Of a humming-bird in June.

I should not have heeded his idle song,
  But his breath was on my face,
And his arms around my neck were flung
  In a fairy-like embrace.

Then "Whither away, sweet wind?" said I,
  "And why is thy song so gay?
And why do thy waving pinions fly
  So busily all the day?"

"Like a child asleep," the zephyr said,
  "I have lain the whole long night,
With the moonbeams spread above my bed,
  For a covering pure and white.

"But, just as the sun from out of the sea
  Had lifted his princely head,
The morn, like a mother, lifted me
  From out of my snowy bed.

"Then up, in the golden light, I flew
  O'er meadow and grassy hills ;
I sprinkled the clover-heads with dew,
  I ruffled the meadow rills ;

"I swept the boughs of the beech aside,
  To look at the nestling birds ;
The broken flower by the rolling tide
  I cheered with my loving words.

"I fluttered afar with the dancing hours,
  O'er forest and creeping vine ;
I gleefully kissed the bending flowers,
  Till their lips were red as wine.

" Oh, swiftly I fly o'er the rustling grass,
  And the wheat on smiling farms,
Till the old nurse Night comes down at last,
  And cradles me in her arms.

" Then whither away ? " said the wind to me,
  " And where hast *thou* been to-day ?
And why is thy face so sad to see,
  When everything else is gay ? "

" Alas ! sweet wind," I sighed to say,
  While the tears in my eyelids grew,
" *I* have not borne to a soul to-day,
  Love's delicate draught of dew.

" I have not searched for the broken flowers
  That wither along the way,
Nor gladdened the flight of the priceless hours,
  Nor bent my knee to pray.

" O, sweet are thy songs o'er lake and lea,
  At the morning and eventide ;
But the lesson of love thou hast taught to me,
  Is sweeter than aught beside."
                        Amanda T. Jones.

OUR MOTHER'S SAMPLER.

It was wrought in silken letters,
  As was the fashion then.
Stitched into our mother's sampler—
  " Eliza, aged Ten ! "
'Twas long ago—passed sixty years !
Below the name the date appears.

In " eighteen hundred twenty-three ! "
  We often heard her tell—
She walked two miles to school that year,
  And we remember well,
How underneath the elm tree's shade
She rested when a little maid.

Above her name the Alphabet,
  In letters large and small,
Was wrought in red, and "true love blue,"
  And cross-stitched, one and all.
The rows divided off by lines,
Made from some old and quaint designs.

And through the Summer sunshine,
  And through the Winter's snow,
With the sampler in her pocket,
  Our mother used to go.
And afternoons, the lessons done,
She worked the letters one by one.

The stitches evenly were set,
  With only here and there
A misplaced one, perhaps the count
  Was lost midst childish care.
Distracting things in school, perchance,
Stole from the work a thought, a glance.

They tell me it was beautiful,
  Our mother's childhood face,
And speak of all her kindly words,
  Her ways of simple grace.
Could we have only seen her then,
That child, "Eliza, aged ten!"

We knew her not at morning:
  But when her noon-time came,
With childish love and prattle,
  We gave her the new name;
Replete with all that's pure and good—
The sacred name of motherhood.

And now the afternoon has passed:
  It is the evening tide;
Our mother has just entered in
  Among the glorified.
We look her finished life-work through—
The misplaced stitches, O how few!
        Susan Teall Perry, in Evangelist.

LITTLE FLORENCE.

O FLORENCE, little Florence,
   With your face so bonny-bright,
With your hair so full of sunshine,
   With your eyes so full of light,

With your head so full of frolic,
   With your heart so full of love,
If you could only tell me,
   Could tell me, pretty dove!

Do the little laughing cherubs
   Slide down the moonbeams white,
And whisper funny stories,
   And talk to you all night?—

The funny bits of ballads
   You babble now and then,
In a sweeter, softer language
   Than other mortals ken.

Do they joke and jest so gleeful,
   From set of sun till dawn,
That you lie and crow and giggle
   Long after they are gone?

Do they always bring two dewy,
   Fresh pieces of the sky,
And lift your lashes softly
   And slip them under sly?

Do they pinch your cheeks a trifle,
   To make the roses blow?
Do they punch your chubby fingers,
   To make the dimples grow?

Do they show you sights of mischief,
   All sorts of things to do
(Just to keep a body busy,
   And the world from getting "blue")?

Do they tickle you at table,
   And tempt you to a spree
(Just to shake the mental cobwebs)
   When the Parson's in to tea?

Do they pity the canary,
   And come to you and say,
'Tis weary of its prison
   And wants to get away?

Do they hint the budding calla
   Is bold enough to bloom,
If some one isn't careful
   To pluck it pretty soon?

Do they tell you on which bushes
   Grows "de bestest zinzerbread"?
That how to get new dollies
   Is to smash the old one's head?

Do they teach you model methods
   For enslaving humankind—
The way to rule the father
   And to make the mother mind?

And to keep all of us people,
   Who live across the street,
Forever on the listen
   For the tinkling of your feet?

Alas! ere you can answer,
   I'm very much in fear
The cherubs will have finished
   A-whispering in your ear.

'Tis cloudy April weather,
   There's a chill in all the air,
And over in the window
   I see the golden hair.

Somebody must stay indoors,
   For fear of catching cold;
And it's "defful" tiresome business
   For little Three-years-old.

But the whole town remembers
 How, not six months agone,
All round the house the curtains
 Were ever closely drawn,

And where erewhile the door-bell
 Its frequent summons rang,
Was pinned a pencilled notice,
 To hush the piercing clang.

For little, little Florence
 Among the shadows lay,
In fever, moaning, tossing,
 The livelong night and day.

And oft was asked the question,
 "Is she any better now?"
With a choking and a tremor
 One couldn't help, somehow.

But *she* does not remember,
 Of course—the blithesome heart.
See! she has donned her "yiding-hood,"
 All ready for a start.

And—now! quick, no one watching,
 Down, down the walk she flies—
And Betsy rushing after,
 With a twinkle in her eyes.

Ha! let us see you catch her—
 The wee Red Riding-hood!
A flash of scarlet lightning;
 She's in a racing mood.

Quick, o'er the muddy crossing
 (The dainty buttoned shoes!)
Quick, quick, around the corner—
 Ah, she begins to lose!

And—now!—the race is over.
 You little midget, you!
To laugh such bubbling laughter,
 The other must laugh too.

And now the door closed on her,
  As yesterday, no doubt—
"Mamma must haf to lock it,
  Or some peoples *vill* get out."

Once, left alone a moment,
  They couldn't find the child;
And the father's face was ghastly,
  And the mother—she went wild.

Nor here, nor there, the missing;
  The neighbors, looking out,
Saw all the household flying
  Promiscuously about,

And joined the search, in terror,
  And hurried to and fro;
"Oh! where—oh! where is Florence?
  Does anybody know?"

"O Florence! Florence! Florence!"
  There came a little squeal
From Pony Prince's manger—
  "I be here in de meal."

The darling! may kind Heaven
  Preserve her safe and sound!
For her ways defy conjecture,
  And her plans—they are profound.

But bless the little cherubs
  Who ride the moonbeams white,
And come to her a-cooing,
  A-cooing all the night!

Who come to her with manna—
  The melting music-mirth
She scatters in her pathway,
  To gladden all the earth.

And bless the little Florence,
  With her face so bonny-bright,
With her hair so full of sunshine,
  With her eyes so full of light!

Aye, bless you, little sunbeam !
Shine on a good long while !
The world will be the better
For the ripple in your smile !
Ellen Tracy Alden.

PRAYERS OF THE CHILDREN.

"Come hither, George and Marion,
Come hither, Isabelle ! "
Far off, the mother's voice, and low,
But on their *hearts* it fell.

And George—the rosy, dark-eyed rogue,
Came bounding at her will ;
And Isabelle—the darling,
And Marion meek and still.

" Now if you each one prayer to Heaven,
And only one, might say,
For what, my precious little ones,
Would you this moment pray ? "

" Oh ! I would pray that God would send
His bright heaven down to earth,
Nor take us from our tender friends,"
Said George, in thoughtless mirth.

" And I," said loving Isabelle,
" Would ask, my darling mother,
That we might go together there—
Thou, Marion, I, and brother."

Then Marion raised her thoughtful eyes—
Our little dreaming nun—
" And thou ? "—Serene the child replies,
" I'd say--Thy will be done ! "
Frances S. Osgood.

BED-TIME.

When the lamps were lit in the evening,
    And the shutters were fastened tight,
And the room where the household gathered
    Was cosy, and warm and bright,
When the bustle of work was over,
    And the children were tired of play,
It seemed to us that our bed-time
    Was the pleasantest part of the day.

For grandmother had her knitting;
    Click! click! would the needles go;
The baby was snug in the cradle,
    And mother had time to sew;
And we in our little night-gowns,
    Would clamber on father's knee,
And sheltered within his loving arms
    Were happy as we could be.

He could not sing; but he whistled
    A tune that was sure to keep
The little ones very quiet,
    And put the baby to sleep;
And whenever I want a lullaby,
    The sweetest I e'er shall know
Is the one that my father always used
    In the beautiful long ago.

Sometimes there were apples roasted,
    And then there were nuts to crack;
And jokes to be told, and stories
    That had a delicious smack;
And the longer we lingered, the harder
    We found it to get away,
For to us the children's bed-time
    Seemed the sweetest hour of the day.

But at last the word was spoken;
    "Come, come!" the mother said,
In her quietest tones,—"it is really time
    That little folks went to bed;"

And we who were wide awake as owls,
   And ready for any lark,
With mournful step moved slowly out
   And into the joyless dark.

And long after we were folded
   In slumber's serene embrace,
And with the angels of dreamland
   Were floating through fairy space,
Dear father would come to our bedside,
   And tuck us in, oh, so tight!
We'd sleep as warm as birds in a nest
   All through the livelong night.

And when my bed-time cometh,
   And the last " Good-nights " are said,
And with the rest of the children
   I go to my narrow bed,
My sleep will be the sweeter
   For the touch of a loving hand,
And a Father's smile will greet me
   As I enter the morning-land.
                    Josephine Pollard.

THE MIGHT OF TRUTH.

WE are proclaimed, even against our wills—
   If we are silent, then our silence speaks—
Children from tumbling on the summer hills
   Come home with roses rooted in their cheeks.
I think no man can make his lie hold good,—
One way or other, truth is understood.

The still sweet influence of a life of prayer
   Quickens their hearts who never bow the knee,—
So come fresh draughts of living inland air
   To weary homesick men, far out at sea.
Acquaint thyself with God, O man, and lo!
His light shall like a garment round thee flow.

The selfishness that with our lives has grown,
  Though outward grace its full expression bar,
Will crop out here and there like belts of stone
  From shallow soil, discovering what we are.
The thing most specious cannot stead the true,—
Who would appear clean, must be clean all through.

Alice Cary

THE BEAUTIFUL HAND.

THREE maidens by the wayside—
So runs an ancient story—
  From idle chat and jest,
Began at length, disputing
  Whose hands were loveliest.

The strife grew hot and bitter,
Until, at last, each yielded
  Thus much of stubborn pride,
To say the first one passing
  Between them should decide.

Then one in crystal water,
Dipped all her pretty fingers
  A dazzling white to gain;
Another gathered strawberries
  To give a rosy stain;

Another in the thicket,
Sought violets white and purple,
  And plucked them for their scent.
Just then an aged woman
  Drew near, so wan, so bent.

Only a feeble beggar,
Faltering and thin and hungry,
  Opening her withered palms
To each in turn, beseeching,
  In quavering tones, for alms.

Close followed a girl, a peasant;
The three, the beggar scorning,
   Of her made quick demand,
Holding their hands before her:—
   "Whose is the loveliest hand?"

She gave them smiling answer:
(But gently thrust a penny—
   More than she well could spare—
First in the beggar's fingers)
   "Oh, all are very fair."

Ah, then what change came over
That bowed and shrivelled figure!
   Full in their dazzled sight
Her faded, tattered garments
   Grew into robes of light.

With soft white wings unfolded,
They saw her lifted, rising,
   Beautiful as a bird,
Up to the sky, while breathless
   With awe, these words they heard:

"The hands of the vain and selfish
Are never fair nor lovely;
   The peasant's are more fair,
For she gave to the Lord's own needy,
   More than she well could spare."

And then they knew that an angel
Had crossed their path and spoken
   In that poor beggar's guise,
And the hard hands of the peasant
   Looked white even to their eyes.
      Mrs. Clara Doty Bates, in Good Cheer.

JUDGE NOT.

JUDGE not; the workings of his brain
   And of his heart thou canst not see;
What looks to thy dim eyes a stain,
   In God's pure light may only be

A scar, brought from some well-worn field,
Where thou wouldst only faint and yield.

The look, the air, that frets thy sight,
   May be a token, that below
The soul has closed in deadly fight
   With some infernal fiery foe,
Whose glance would scorch thy smiling grace,
And cast thee shuddering on thy face!

The fall thou darest to despise—
   May be the angel's slackened hand
Has suffered it, that he may rise
   And take a firmer, surer stand.
Or, trusting less to earthly things,
May henceforth *learn* to use his wings.

And judge none lost; but wait and see,
   With hopeful pity, not disdain,
The depth of the abyss may be
   The measure of the height of pain,
And love and glory, that may raise
This soul to God in after days.
               Adelaide Anne Proctor.

SONG OF MARION'S MEN.

Our band is few, but true and tried,
   Our leader frank and bold;
The British soldier trembles
   When Marion's name is told.
Our fortress is the good greenwood,
   Our tent the cypress tree;
We know the forest round us,
   As seamen know the sea;
We know its walls of thorny vines
   Its glades of reedy grass,
Its safe and silent islands
   Within the dark morass.

Woe to the English soldiery
   That little dread us near!
On them shall light at midnight
   A strange and sudden fear,
When, waking to their tents on fire,
   They grasp their arms in vain,
And they who stand to free us
   Are beat to earth again;
And they who fly in terror deem
   A mighty host behind,
And hear the tramp of thousands
   Upon the hollow wind.

Then sweet the hour that brings release
   From danger and from toil;
We talk the battle over,
   And share the battle's spoil.
The woodland rings with laugh and shout,
   As if a hunt were up,
And woodland flowers are gathered
   To crown the soldier's cup.
With merry songs we mock the wind
   That in the pine-top grieves,
And slumber long and sweetly
   On beds of oaken leaves.

Well knows the fair and friendly moon
   The band that Marion leads,—
The glitter of their rifles,
   The scampering of their steeds.
'Tis life to guide the fiery barb
   Across the moonlight plain;
'Tis life to feel the night-wind
   That lifts his tossing mane.
A moment in the British camp—
   A moment—and away
Back to the pathless forest
   Before the peep of day.

Grave men there are by broad Santee,
   Grave men with hoary hairs;
Their hearts are all with Marion,
   For Marion are their prayers.

And lovely ladies greet our band
　　With kindliest welcoming,
With smiles like those of summer,
　　And tears like those of spring.
For them we wear these trusty arms,
　　And lay them down no more
Till we have driven the Briton
　　Forever from our shore.
　　　　　　　　Wm. Cullen Bryant.

THE RELIEF OF LUCKNOW.

OH that last day in Lucknow fort!
　　We knew that it was the last,
That the enemy's lines crept surely on,
　　And the end was coming fast.

To yield to that foe was worse than death,
　　And the men and we all worked on;
It was one day more of smoke and war,
　　And then it would all be done.

There was one of us, a corporal's wife,
　　A fair, young, gentle thing,
Wasted with fever in the siege
　　And her mind was wandering.

She lay on the ground in her Scottish plaid,
　　And I took her head on my knee:
"When my father comes hame frae the pleugh,"
　　she said,
　　"Oh! then please wauken me."

She slept like a child on her father's floor
　　In the flecking of woodbine shade,
When the house-dog sprawls by the open
　　door,
　　And the mother's wheel is staid.

It was smoke and roar and powder-stench,
   And hopeless waiting for death;
And the soldier's wife, like a full-tired child,
   Seemed scarcely to draw her breath.

I sank to sleep, and I had my dream
   Of an English village-lane,
And wall and garden;—but one wild scream
   Brought me back to the roar again.

There Jessie Brown stood listening,
   Till a sudden gladness broke
All over her face, and she caught my hand,
   And drew me near as she spoke:—

"The Hielanders! Oh! dinna ye hear
   The slogan far awa'?
The McGregors! Oh! I ken it weel,
   It's the grandest o' them a'!

"God bless the bonny Hielanders!
   We're saved! we're saved!" she cried;
And fell on her knees, and thanks to God
   Flowed forth like a full flood-tide.

Along the battery-line her cry
   Had fallen among the men,   [die;
And they started back;—they were there to
   But was life so near them, then?

They listened for life; the rattling fire
   Far off, and the far-off roar,
Were all; and the colonel shook his head,
   And they turned to their guns once more.

But Jessie said, "The slogan's done;
   But winna ye hear it noo?
The Campbells are comin'! It's nae a dream;
   Our succors hae broken through!"

We heard the roar and the rattle afar,
   But the pipes we could not hear;
So the men plied their work of hopeless war,
   And knew that the end was near.

It was not long ere it made its way,—
A shrilling ceaseless sound :
It was no noise from the strife afar,
Or the sappers underground.

It *was* the pipes of the Highlanders !
And now they played " Auld Lang Syne ; "
It came to our men like the voice of God,
And they shouted along the line.

And they wept, and shook one another's hands,
And the women sobbed in a crowd ;
And every one knelt down where he stood,
And we all thanked God aloud.

That happy time when we welcomed them,
Our men put Jessie first ;
And the general gave her his hand, and cheers
Like a storm from the soldiers burst.

And the pipers' ribbons and tartans streamed,
Marching round and round our line :
And our joyful cheers were broken with tears
As the pipers played Auld Lang Syne.
Robert Lowell.

PERSEVERANCE.

A swallow in the spring
Came to our granary, and 'neath the eaves
Essayed to make a nest, and there did bring
Wet straw and earth and leaves.

Day after day she toiled
With patient art, but ere her work was crowned,
Some sad mishap the tiny fabric spoiled,
And dashed it to the ground.

She found the ruin wrought,
But not cast down, forth from the place she
    flew,
And with her mate fresh earth and grasses
    brought
    And built her nest anew.

But scarcely had she placed
The last soft feather on its ample floor,
When wicked hand, or chance, again laid
    waste
    And wrought the ruin o'er.

But still her heart she kept,
And toiled again,—and last night, hearing
    calls,
I looked,—and lo! three little swallows slept
    Within the earth-made walls.

What truth is here, O man!
Hath hope been smitten in its early dawn?
Have clouds o'ercast thy purpose, trust or
    plan?
    Have faith, and struggle on!
                                R. S. S. Andros.

THE HERITAGE.

The rich man's son inherits lands,
   And piles of brick, and stone, and gold,
And he inherits soft, white hands,
   And tender flesh that feels the cold,
   Nor dares to wear a garment old;
A heritage, it seems to me,
One scarce would wish to hold in fee.

The rich man's son inherits cares;
   The bank may break, the factory burn,
A breath may burst his bubble shares,
   And soft, white hands could hardly earn
   A living that would serve his turn;
A heritage, it seems to me,
One scarce would wish to hold in fee.

The rich man's son inherits wants,
   His stomach craves for dainty fare;
With sated heart, he hears the pants
   Of toiling hinds with brown arms bare,
   And wearies in his easy chair;
A heritage, it seems to me,
One scarce would wish to hold in fee.

What doth the poor man's son inherit?
   Stout muscles and a sinewy heart,
A hardy frame, a hardier spirit;
   King of two hands, he does his part
   In every useful toil and art;
A heritage, it seems to me,
A king might wish to hold in fee.

What doth the poor man's son inherit?
   Wishes o'erjoyed with humble things,
A rank adjudged by toil-worn merit,
   Content that from employment springs,
   A heart that in his labor sings;
A heritage, it seems to me,
A king might wish to hold in fee.

What doth the poor man's son inherit?
 A patience learned by being poor,
Courage, if sorrow come, to bear it,
 A fellow-feeling that is sure
 To make the outcast bless his door;
A heritage, it seems to me,
A king might wish to hold in fee.

O rich man's son! there is a toil,
 That with all others level stands;
Large charity doth never soil,
 But only whiten, soft, white hands,—
 This is the best crop from thy lands;
A heritage, it seems to me,
Worth being rich to hold in fee.

O poor man's son! scorn not thy state;
 There is worse weariness than thine,
In merely being rich and great;
 Toil only gives the soul to shine,
 And makes rest fragrant and benign;
A heritage, it seems to me,
Worth being poor to hold in fee.

Both, heirs to some six feet of sod,
 Are equal in the earth at last;
Both, children of the same dear God,
 Prove title to your heirship vast
 By record of a well-filled past;
A heritage, it seems to me,
Well worth a life to hold in fee.
James Russell Lowell.

THE NURSE'S SONG.

WHEN nursery lamps are veiled, and nurse is singing
 In accents low,
Timing her music to the cradle's swinging,
 Now fast, now slow—

Singing of Baby Bunting, soft and furry
    In rabbit cloak,
Or rock-a-byed amid the toss and flurry
    Of wind-swept oak;

Of Boy Blue, sleeping with his horn beside him;
    Of my son John,
Who went to bed (let all good boys deride him)
    With stockings on;

Of sweet Bo-Peep, following her lambkins straying;
    Of Dames in shoes;
Of cows, considerate, 'mid the Piper's playing,
    Which tune to choose;

Of Gotham's wise men bowling o'er the billow,
    Or him, less wise,
Who chose rough bramble-bushes for a pillow,
    And scratched his eyes.

It may be, while she sings, that through the portal
    Soft footsteps glide,
And, all invisible to grown-up mortal,
    At cradle side

Sits Mother Goose herself, the dear old mother,
    And rocks and croons,
In tones which Baby hearkens, but no other,
    Her old-new tunes!

I think it must be so, else why, years after,
    Do we retrace
And sing with shadowy recollected laughter,
    Thoughts of that face;

Seen, yet unseen, beaming across the ages
    Brimful of fun
And wit and wisdom, baffling all the sages
    Under the sun?

A grown-up child has place still, which no other
. May dare refuse,
I, grown-up, bring this offering to our Mother,
To Mother Goose.

And standing with the babies at that olden,
Immortal knee,
I seem to feel her smile, benign and golden,
Falling on me.
Susan Coolidge.

APPLE BLOSSOMS.

I LEAN from my eastward window
To the kiss of the morning fair,
And a joy in my heart too full for words,
Springs up at the matin hymn of the birds,
Thrilling the tremulous air.

The brown of the winding roadway
Is bound with ribbons of green;
Beyond is the stretch of the grassy leas,
And the blossoming boughs of the orchard trees
Are rosy and white between.

An ocean of scented billows,
They sway to the breath of spring,—
With many a craft of new-built nest,
Rocking at anchor upon their breast,
Its pennant a flashing wing.

Hark! Clearer than note of robin,
A song to my window comes!
'Tis Alice, crowned with a garland sweet,
Who sings, to the beat of her gladsome feet,
This lay of the apple blooms:

"Tell me, Apple Blossoms,
   How your robes were made!
Did the fairies weave them
   In the grassy glade,
Out of threads of sunshine,
   On a magic loom,—
Paint them with the morning,
   Dip them in perfume?

"Or, when May looked northward,
   To the waiting land,
And stern winter, frowning,
   Raised his icy hand,
Did the wall of snow-flakes
   That he fain would pile,
Turn to drifting blossoms
   Underneath her smile?

"Tell me, Apple Blossoms!
   Do not trust the bee!
He will buzz the secret
   Ere he leaves the tree.
Butterflies are fickle,
   Humming birds so proud!
Tell me, Apple Blossoms,—
   Do not speak aloud!"

O Alice! My love, my darling!
   If the Apple Blossoms could speak,
The beautiful secret they fain would tell,
Were not of their colors that match so well
   The tint of your glowing cheek!

When the rose-white petals have fallen,
   And their delicate fragrance has fled,
What is it will grow through the summer noons,
And ripen under calm harvest moons
   In the place of the flower that is dead?

So the beautiful face of my darling
  May fade and be hidden some day,
But the fair white soul that God's breath
    has given,
Unblighted shall grow through the summer of heaven:—
  This the Apple Blossoms would say.
           Mary A. P. Humphrey.

BABY-LAND.

How many miles to Baby-Land?
  Any one can tell;
    Up one flight,
    To your right—
  Please to ring the bell.

What can you see in Baby-Land?
  Little folks in white,
    Downy heads.
    Cradle-beds,
  Faces pure and bright.

What do they do in Baby-Land?
  Dream and wake and play,
    Laugh and crow,
    Shout and grow;
  Jolly times have they.

What do they say in Baby-Land?
  Why, the oddest things;
    Might as well
    Try to tell
  What a birdie sings.

Who is the queen of Baby-Land?
  Mother; kind and sweet;
    And her love,
    Born above,
  Guides the little feet.
           George Cooper.

A CENTENNIAL TEA-POT.

GREAT-GREAT-GRANDMOTHER, Winifred Lee,
Brought, when she came across the sea,
A porcelain tea-pot pictured o'er,
After a fashion they knew of yore,
Bright with birds and with summer flowers
And fairies dancing in shady bowers—
A pretty treasure to keep in mind
The pleasant home she had left behind.

Weeks of battle with storm and gale
Wore on timber and mast and sail,
And just a league from its destined goal
The ship was wrecked on a sudden shoal.
Rescued, the people sped to shore,
Saving their lives and nothing more.

But Winifred, pacing the beach next day,
Dreaming of England far away—
A little homesick and lone and sad,
In spite of the morning gay and glad—
Saw, as she strolled, how the thriving tide
Had brought its plunder and scattered wide,
And beheld, in seaweed carefully wound,
The porcelain tea-pot safe and sound!

When years had passed and the King's demand
Roused the people of all the land,
And a ship's cargo was put away
To steep at the bottom of Boston Bay,
With a rebel heart and a flashing eye
Winifred laid her tea-pot by;
"Till we are granted our rights," said she,
"I'll drink not another cup of tea."

(Oh, matrons of this luxurious age,
Who lightly turn from History's page,
Just for a year or two forego
Your redolent draughts of rare Pekoe,
And say if you deem the self-denial
Of our great-great-grandmothers not a trial!)

Murder, and pillage, and cannon's roar,
All along the Connecticut shore,
Frighted from town the worthy dame.
Next day a barrack her house became,
And a troop of Redcoats helped themselves
To all they could find on the pantry shelves.
They drank and feasted, and sang and swore,
They tumbled the beds and the curtains tore,
And the quiet, orderly, well-kept house
Was the scene of a livelong night's carouse.

Homeward stealing when they had passed,
Winifred gazed at the sight aghast.
With wrecks of revel the floors were strewn,
With tables broken and chairs o'erthrown;
Delicate saucer, and cup, and plate,
Ruined all—but, strange to relate,
The porcelain tea-pot standing still,
Safe and sound, on a window-sill!

Long and long have the lichens grown,
Wreathing a slender slab of stone,
Till scarcely the letters can you see
That spell the name of Winifred Lee.
But the pictured porcelain, handed down,
Far from the old elm-shaded town,
An heirloom prized, had found retreat
High over a thronged Chicago street—
There, in its corner, fresh and gay
As tho' it were made but yesterday.

When in the night a terror came,
And the great city was red with flame,
And the people, jostling, gasped for breath
As they wildly fled from the jaws of death;
Little leisure or care had they
Their household treasures to bear away.

Nevertheless, as one returned
To where the *débris* smouldering burned,
Where heaps of ashes, and brick, and stone,
Were all that remained of a goodly home—
Saving a charred and blackened wall,
Like skeleton rising gaunt and tall—
Glancing upward, with wondering eye,
The marvelous tea-pot did he spy,
Boldly gleaming against the sky.

Ah, old tea-pot, gleaming still,
What is the magic that guards from ill,
From tempest, and war, and time, and fire—
All for thy ruin that conspire?
Behold thee, shining so bright and gay!
Old tea-pot, art thou bewitched, I say?
If that be true, and in some hour
Thou should'st possess thee of speech the
    power,
With the vapor that curls from thy graceful
    spout
What prisoned secret wilt thou let out?
Wilt tell how gossips have lisped and chided
At little suppers where thou hast presided?
Wilt ever laugh at the fortunes told,
The willing credence of young and old,
As the sibylline leaves thou didst unfold?

Forsooth, as I watch thee blink and shine
In that remarkable way of thine,
I'm half afraid of thee!—No, not so,
Thou precious relic of long ago!

Breathing fragrance and friendly cheer,
Live for many and many a year!
The next Centennial may'st thou see,
Is the toast I drink in a cup of tea.
Ellen Tracy Alden.

WORDS.

WORDS are lighter than the cloud-foam
   Of the restless ocean spray;
Vainer than the trembling shadow
   That the next hour steals away.
By the fall of summer rain-drops
   Is the air as deeply stirred;
And the rose-leaf that we tread on
   Will outlive a word.

Yet, on the dull silence breaking
   With a lightning flash, a Word,
Bearing endless desolation
   On its blighting wings, I heard;
Earth can forge no keener weapon
   Dealing surer death and pain,
And the cruel echo answered
   Through long years again.

I have known one word hang star-like
   O'er a dreary waste of years,
And it only shone the brighter
   Looked at through a mist of tears;
While a weary wanderer gathered
   Hope and heart on Life's dark way,
By its faithful promise-shining
   Clearer day by day.

I have known a spirit, calmer
   Than the calmest lake, and clear
As the heavens that gazed upon it,
   With no wave of hope or fear;

But a storm had swept across it,
  And its deepest depths were stirred,
(Never, never more to slumber,)
  Only by a word.

I have known a word more gentle
  Than the breath of summer air;
In a listening heart it nestled,
  And it lived forever there.
Not the beating of its prison
  Stirred it ever, night or day,
Only with the heart's last throbbing
  Could it fade away.

Words are mighty, words are living;
  Serpents with their venomous stings,
Or bright angels crowding round us,
  With heaven's light upon their wings.
Every word has its own spirit,
  True or false, that never dies;
Every word man's lips have uttered,
  Echoes in God's skies.
              Adelaide Anne Proctor.

LITTLE HARRY AND THE NEW MOON.

"Pretty new moon,
    How do you do?
Long I've been looking,
    And looking for you!
Where have you hid yourself,
    'Way off so far?
Or did you get lost,
    Like the wandering star?

"My mamma undressed me,
    And now off she goes;
She kisses and leaves me,
    And nobody knows

How sad and how frightened
　I feel here alone,
Except when you're shining,
　You pretty new moon.

"I like to lie watching
　Your bright little boat,
That seems on the sky
　So smoothly to float;
And then every evening,
　To watch how you grow,
Getting bigger and bigger,
　Till again off you go.

"If you only would tell me,
　You pretty new moon,
Whereabouts you are living,
　And where you are gone
When you hide away from me,
　For many a week;
If you only would tell me—
　Pretty moon, won't you speak?"

"'Tis a wonderful story,
　My dear little boy;
I cannot half tell you,
　My work and my joy.
The dear God has made me
　And hung me on high,
To shine in the evening
　And light up the sky.

"I hang where he bids me,
　And roll on the line
Marked out by his finger,
　And do naught but shine.
The sunlight falls on me,
　Wherever I go,
And then I'm so happy
　I smile upon you.

"Sometimes I roll near you
   While 'tis yet afternoon,
Just one edge you see then,
   And call me new moon;
But when I get larger
   I shine all the night,
And give the grown-up folks
   My pretty, soft light.

"Suppose now, I pouted,
   And hung down my head,
And wouldn't be happy,
   Or do as I'm bid;
And shook off the sunbeams
   That wanted to fall,
And covered my face
   With a gloomy black pall."

Little Harry was frightened,
   And crouched down in bed,
To think that the new moon
   Had seen what he did!
For he had been naughty,
   Had pouted and frowned,
Though all things were pleasant
   And smiling around.

He had not minded mamma,
   Nor gone, as she said,
Contented to supper,
   And then off to bed;
And now, to find out
   That the pretty new moon
Had seen his bad conduct,
   And told it so soon!

He hid in the bed-clothes,
   Ashamed and afraid,
And, while he lay there,
   This is just what he said:

"Pretty moon, from this moment
  I'll always obey,
With a bright smiling face,
  And will mind right away."
                    Helen E. Brown.

THE STORY OF MOTHER BECKER.

[Mrs. Abigail Becker, who lived upon a little island near the foot of Lake Erie, saved the crew of the schooner "Conductor" from death, November, 1854.]

"AWAKE!" cried Mother Becker, "wake,
  My children one and all:
For there's a wreck upon the lake—
  I heard the sailors call;
And you must keep the cabin warm,
  And safe from wind and frost;
Unless I save them from the storm
  Their lives will all be lost."

Up sprang the children from their beds—
  Her seven girls and boys;
The blast was shrieking o'er their heads,
  The air was full of noise;
The waves with driven foam were crowned,
  Far flew the freezing spray;
They saw the schooner lie aground,
  Full half a mile away.

Across a sandy bar at night,
  Hard beaten by the gale—
Her leaky hull had sunk from sight,
  And torn was every sail.
But, in the sleety air, each mast
  Still to and fro was swung
And, to the icy shrouds made fast,
  Seven weary sailors clung.

In haste ran Mother Becker then!
    What cared she for the cold,
If aught could aid those freezing men,
    Out where the waters rolled?
"Now if I had a boat," said she,
    "In spite of wind and wave,
I'd row across this plunging sea,
    Their precious lives to save."

She looked afar to left and right,
    Along the sandy wall,
But not a boat was there in sight—
    The tide had loosed them all.
She looked toward the further beach
    Half hidden with the spray;
But not a man the isle could reach,
    Through all that wintry day.

Beside the raging lake she stood,
    And many a sign she made;
"Leap down and swim the angry flood—
    O, do not be afraid!"
The captain saw—"My men," he cried,
    "Her signals let us trust;
I'll be the first to brave the tide
    And drown—if drown we must."

He plunged among the boiling waves,
    On, toward the sandy shore
He swam—above the sailors' graves,
    Who had been wrecked before,
Almost to land his way he urged,
    When, rolling broad and free,
A backward billow o'er him surged
    And tossed him out to sea!

Haste, mother Becker! see! he drowns!
    She rushes out to save,
A foamy crest above her frowns—
    She battles with the wave.

On to his aid she presses fast;
    He sinks—his strength is o'er;
She grasps him in her arms at last,
    She bears him safe to shore.

She hears beyond the sandy bar
    The waiting sailors' cheer;
She smiles, she beckons from afar,
    "Plunge in and do not fear!"
Against their feet the tide is rolled—
    They shudder on the brink;
They faint with hunger and with cold;
    But not a man will shrink.

And one by one, across the lake,
    They try the foaming track;
Till flung from shore, the billows break,
    And whirl them, helpless, back,
And still as, one by one, the crew
    Go down with gasping breath,
Brave mother Becker struggles through
    And snatches them frem death.

Her freezing raiment round her clings,
    Her bare feet print the sand;
But, toiling, panting, lo, she brings
    The last man safe to land.
In from the howling of the storm,
    That fills the world with noise,
She leads them to her cabin warm,
    Among her girls and boys.

The smoking meal was ready set,
    A merry fire they had;
Dear mother Becker, never yet
    Were boys and girls so glad!
And for your sake, on land or sea,
    O, woman strong to save,
May all your seven children be
    As noble and as brave!

Amanda T. Jones.

CHRIST AND THE LITTLE ONES.

"THE Master has come over Jordan,"
   Said Hannah the mother one day;
"He is healing the people who throng him
   With a touch of His finger, they say.

"And now I shall carry the children,
   Little Rachel, and Samuel, and John,
I shall carry the baby, Esther,
   For the Lord to look upon."

The father looked at her kindly,
   But he shook his head and smiled:
"Now who but a doting mother
   Would think of a thing so wild?

"If the children were tortured by demons,
   Or dying of fever 'twere well;
Or had they the taint of the leper,
   Like many in Israel."

"Nay, do not hinder me, Nathan;
   I feel such a burden of care;
If I carry it to my Master
   Perhaps I shall leave it there.

"If He lay His hand on the children,
   My heart will be lighter, I know;
For a blessing forever and ever
   Will follow them as they go."

So over the hills of Judea,
   Along by the vine-rows green,
With Esther asleep on her bosom,
   And Rachel her brothers between;

'Mid the people who hung on His teaching,
  Or waited His touch and His Word,
Through the row of proud Pharisees listening
  She pressed to the feet of the Lord.

"Now why shouldst thou hinder the Master,"
  Said Peter, "with children like these!
Seest not how, from morning to evening
  He teacheth and healeth disease?"

Then Christ said, "Forbid not the children,
  Permit them to come unto me!"
And He took to His arms little Esther,
  And Rachel He set on His knee;

And the heavy heart of the mother
  Was lifted all earth-care above,
As He laid His hand on the brothers,
  And blessed them with tenderest love;

As He said of the babes in His bosom:
"Of such is the Kingdom of Heaven;"
And strength for all duty and trial
  That hour to her spirit was given.
            Julia Gill.

PAUL REVERE'S RIDE.

LISTEN, my children, and you shall hear
Of the midnight ride of Paul Revere,
On the eighteenth of April, in Seventy-five;
Hardly a man is now alive
Who remembers that famous day and year.

He said to his friend, "If the British march
By land or sea from the town to-night,
Hang a lantern aloft in the belfry arch
Of the North Church tower as a signal light,
One, if by land, and two, if by sea;

And I on the opposite shore will be,
Ready to ride and spread the alarm
Through every Middlesex village and farm,
For the country folk to be up and to arm."

Then he said, "Good-night!" and with muffled oar
Silently rowed to the Charlestown shore,
Just as the moon rose over the bay,
Where swinging wide at her moorings lay
The Somerset, British man-of-war;
A phantom ship, with each mast and spar
Across the moon like a prison bar,
And a huge black hulk, that was magnified
By its own reflection in the tide.

Meanwhile, his friend, through alley and street,
Wanders and watches with eager ears,
Till in the silence around him he hears
The muster of men at the barrack door,
The sound of arms, and the tramp of feet,
And the measured tread of the grenadiers,
Marching down to their boats on the shore.

Then he climbed the tower of the Old North Church,
By the wooden stairs with stealthy tread,
To the belfry-chamber overhead,
And startled the pigeons from their perch
On the sombre rafters that round him made
Masses and moving shapes of shade,—
By the trembling ladder, steep and tall,
To the highest window in the wall,
Where he paused to listen and look down
A moment on the roofs of the town,
And the moonlight flowing over all.

Beneath, in the churchyard, lay the dead,
In their night-encampment on the hill,

Wrapped in silence so deep and still
That he could hear, like a sentinel's tread,
The watchful night-wind as it went
Creeping along from tent to tent,
And seeming to whisper, "All is well!"
A moment only he feels the spell
Of the place and the hour, and the secret dread
Of the lonely belfry and the dead;
For suddenly all his thoughts are bent
On a shadowy something far away,
Where the river widens to meet the bay,
A line of black that bends and floats
On the rising tide, like a bridge of boats.

Meanwhile, impatient to mount and ride,
Booted and spurred, with a heavy stride
On the opposite shore walked Paul Revere.
Now he patted his horse's side,
Now gazed at the landscape far and near,
Then, impetuous, stamped the earth,
And turned and tightened his saddle-girth;
But mostly he watched with eager search
The belfry-tower of the Old North Church,
As it rose above the graves on the hill,
Lonely and spectral and sombre and still.
And lo! as he looks, on the belfry's height
A glimmer, and then a gleam of light!
He springs to the saddle, the bridle he turns,
But lingers and gazes, till full on his sight
A second lamp in the belfry burns!

A hurry of hoofs in a village street,
A shape in the moonlight, a bulk in the dark,
And beneath, from the pebbles, in passing, a
    spark
Struck out by a steed flying fearless and fleet;
That was all! And yet, through the gloom and
    the light,
The fate of a nation was riding that night;

And the spark struck out by the steed in his flight,
Kindled the land into flame with its heat.

He has left the village, and mounted the steep,
And beneath him, tranquil and broad and deep,
Is the Mystic, meeting the ocean tides;
And under the alders that skirt its edge,
Now soft on the sand, now loud on the ledge,
Is heard the tramp of his steed as he rides.

It was twelve by the village clock
When he crossed the bridge into Medford town.
He heard the crowing of the cock,
And the barking of the farmer's dog,
And felt the damp of the river fog,
That rises after the sun goes down.

It was one by the village clock,
When he galloped into Lexington.
He saw the gilded weathercock
Swim in the moonlight as he passed,
And the meeting-house windows, blank and bare,
Gaze at him with a spectral glare,
As if they already stood aghast
At the bloody work they would look upon.

It was two by the village clock,
When he came to the bridge in Concord town.
He heard the bleating of the flock,
And the twitter of birds among the trees,
And felt the breath of the morning breeze
Blowing over the meadows brown.
And one was safe and asleep in his bed
Who at the bridge would be first to fall,
Who that day would be lying dead,
Pierced by a British musket-ball.

You know the rest. In the books you have
    read,
How the British Regulars fired and fled,—
How the farmers gave them ball for ball,
From behind each fence and farm-yard wall,
Chasing the red-coats down the lane,
Then crossing the fields to emerge again
Under the trees at the turn of the road,
And only pausing to fire and load.

So through the night rode Paul Revere;
And so through the night went his cry of
    alarm
To every Middlesex village and farm,—
A cry of defiance and not of fear,
A voice in the darkness, a knock at the door,
And a word that shall echo evermore!

For, borne on the night-wind of the Past,
Through all our history, to the last,
In the hour of darkness and peril and need,
The people will waken and listen to hear
The hurrying hoof-beats of that steed,
And the midnight message of Paul Revere.
                    Henry W. Longfellow.

THE OLD CONTINENTALS.

In their ragged regimentals
Stood the old continentals,
        Yielding not,
When the grenadiers were lunging,
And like hail fell the plunging
        Cannon-shot;
        When the files
        Of the isles,

From the smoky night encampment,
   bore the banner of the rampant
      Unicorn,
And grummer, grummer, grummer,
   rolled the roll of the drummer,
      Through the morn!

Then with eyes to the front all,
And with guns horizontal,
      Stood our sires;
And the balls whistled deadly,
And in streams flashing redly
      Blazed the fires;
         As the roar
         On the shore
Swept the strong battle-breakers o'er
   the green-sodded acres
      Of the plain;
And louder, louder, louder, cracked
   the black gunpowder,
      Cracking amain!

Now like smiths at their forges
Worked the red St. George's
      Cannoneers;
And the "villainous saltpetre"
Rung a fierce discordant metre
      Round their ears;
         As the swift
         Storm-drift
With hot sweeping anger, came the
   horse-guards' clangor
      On our flanks.
Then higher, higher, higher, burned
   the old-fashioned fire
      Through the ranks!

Then the old-fashioned colonel
Galloped through the white infernal
      Powder-cloud;

And his broad sword was swinging
And his brazen throat was ringing
   Trumpet loud.
   Then the blue
   Bullets flew,
And the trooper-jackets redden at the
   touch of the leaden
   Rifle-breath;
And rounder, rounder, rounder, roared
   the iron six-pounder,
   Hurling death!
        Guy Humphrey McMaster.

WAIT!

WHEN a thought comes to your brain
That would place on life a stain,
Crush it out from heart and mind;
For a purer thought to find,
        Wait!

When your lips in haste would speak
Words that show a judgment weak,
Through a passion that would blind,
Or an impulse yet unkind,
        Wait!

When a deed you fain would do,
That you might have cause to rue,
Till the shadows flee your mind,
Hands withhold; to calm your mind,
        Wait!

Wait to passion all subdue;
Wait for loving thought and true;
Wait till lips breathe tender word,
For deeds by gentle impulse stirred.
        Wait!
    Ward Steele, in " The Pansy."

KING CANUTE.

KING CANUTE was weary-hearted; he had reigned for years a score,
Battling, struggling, pushing, fighting, killing much and robbing more;
And he thought upon his actions, walking by the wild sea-shore.

'Twixt the Chancellor and Bishop, walked the King with steps sedate,
Chamberlains and grooms came after, silver-sticks and gold-sticks great,
Chaplains, aides-de-camp and pages,—all the officers of state.

Sliding after like his shadow, pausing when he chose to pause,
If a frown his face contracted, straight the courtiers dropped their jaws;
If to laugh the king was minded, out they burst in loud hee-haws.

But that day a something vexed him; that was clear to old and young;
Thrice His Grace had yawned at table when his favorite gleemen sung,
Once the Queen would have consoled him, but he bade her hold her tongue.

"Something ails my gracious master!" cried the Keeper of the Seal,
"Sure, my lord, it is the lampreys served for dinner, or the veal?"
"Psha!" exclaimed the angry monarch, "Keeper, 't is not that I feel.

"'T is the *heart*, and not the dinner, fool, that
    doth my rest impair;
Can a king be great as I am, prithee, and yet
    know no care?
Oh, I 'm sick, and tired, and weary." Some
    one cried: "The King's arm-chair!"

Then toward the lackeys turning, quick my
    lord the Keeper nodded,
Straight the King's great chair was brought
    him, by two footmen able-bodied;
Languidly he sank into it; it was comfortably
    wadded.

"Leading on my fierce companions," cried he,
    "over storm and brine,
I have fought and I have conquered! Where
    was glory like to mine?"
Loudly all the courtiers echoed: "Where is
    glory like to thine!"

"What avail me all my kingdoms? Weary
    am I now and old;
Those fair sons I have begotten long to see me
    dead and cold;
Would I were, and quiet buried, underneath
    the silent mold!

"Oh, remorse, the writhing serpent! at my
    bosom tears and bites;
Horrid, horrid things I look on, though I put
    out all the lights;
Ghosts of ghastly recollections troop about
    my bed at nights.

"Cities burning, convents blazing, red with
    sacrilegious fires;
Mothers weeping, virgins screaming vainly
    for their slaughtered sires."
"Such a tender conscience," cries the Bishop,
    "every one admires."

"Look, the land is crowned with minsters
  which your Grace's bounty raised;
Abbeys filled with holy men, where you and
  Heaven are daily praised;
You, my lord, to think of dying? on my
  conscience, I 'm amazed!"

"Nay, I feel," replied King Canute, "that my
  end is drawing near."
"Don't say so!" exclaimed the courtiers
  (striving each to squeeze a tear).
"Sure your Grace is strong and lusty, and
  may live this fifty year."

"Live these fifty years!" the Bishop roared,
  with actions made to suit.
"Are you mad, my good Lord Keeper, thus
  to speak of King Canute!
Men have lived a thousand years, and sure
  His Majesty will do 't.

"Adam, Enoch, Lamech, Cainan, Mahaleel,
  Methusela
Lived nine hundred years apiece, and may n't
  the king as well as they?"
"Fervently," exclaimed the Keeper,—
  "fervently I trust he may."

"*He* to die?" resumed the Bishop. "He a
  mortal like to *us*?
Death was not for him intended, though
  communis omnibus; *
Keeper, you are irreligious for to talk and
  cavil thus.

"With his wondrous skill in healing ne'er a
  doctor can compete,
Loathsome lepers, if he touch them, start up
  clean upon their feet;
Surely he could raise the dead up, did His
  Highness think it meet.

---
* Meaning: Common to all.

"Did not once the Jewish captain stay the sun
    upon the hill,
And the while he slew the foemen, bid the
    silver moon stand still?
So, no doubt, could gracious Canute, if it were
    his sacred will."

"Might I stay the sun above us, good Sir
    Bishop?" Canute cried;
"Could I bid the silver moon to pause upon
    her heavenly ride?
If the moon obeys my orders, sure I can
    command the tide!

"Will the advancing waves obey me, Bishop,
    if I make the sign?"
Said the Bishop, bowing lowly: "Land and
    sea, my lord, are thine."
Canute turned toward the ocean: "Back!"
    he said, "thou foaming brine.

"From the sacred shore I stand on, I com-
    mand thee to retreat;
Venture not, thou stormy rebel, to approach
    thy master's seat;
Ocean, be thou still! I bid thee come not
    nearer to my feet!"

But the sullen ocean answered with a louder,
    deeper roar,
And the rapid waves drew nearer, falling
    sounding on the shore;
Back the Keeper and the Bishop, back the
    King and courtiers bore.

And he sternly bade them never more to kneel
    to human clay,
But alone to praise and worship That which
    earth and seas obey;
And his golden crown of empire never wore
    he from that day.

King Canute is dead and gone. Parasites
exist alway.
William Makepeace Thackeray.

A LITTLE PHILOSOPHER.

THE days are short and the nights are long,
  And the wind is nipping cold;
The tasks are hard and the sums are wrong,
  And the teachers often scold.
    But Johnny McCree,
    Oh, what cares he,
  As he whistles along the way?
    " It will all come right
    By to-morrow night,"
  Says Johnny McCree to-day.

The plums are few and the cake is plain,
  The shoes are out at the toe;
For money you look in the purse in vain—
  It was all spent long ago.
    But Johnny McCree,
    Oh, what cares he,
  As he whistles along the street?
    Would you have the blues
    For a pair of shoes,
  While you have a pair of feet?

The snow is deep, there are paths to break,
  But the little arm is strong,
And work is play if you'll only take
  Your work with a bit of song.
    And Johnny McCree,
    Oh, what cares he,
  As he whistles along the road?
    He will do his best,
    And will leave the rest
  To the care of his Father, God.

The mother's face is often sad,
　She scarce knows what to do;
But at Johnny's kiss she is bright and glad—
　She loves him, and wouldn't you?
　　　For Johnny McCree,
　　　Oh, what cares he,
　　As he whistles along the way?
　　　The trouble will go,
　　　And "I told you so,"
　　Our brave little John will say.
　　　　　　Margaret E. Sangster.

ARACHNE.

The garret crowds beneath the roof
　With rafters dusty-brown,
And like a ringing horse's hoof
　All day the rain comes down;
The jagged beams are scarred and stained
　With many a turn and twist;
The two high windows, diamond-paned,
　Are dim with circling mist.

The heavy oaken casement shuts
　Against the rocking wind,
And on the sill the rusty nuts
　Grow sweeter in the rind;
Above the crooked wooden stair
　Are idly hanging still
The anise and the lavender,
　The basil and the dill.

The wide old-fashioned quilting-bars,
　A dozen years gone by,
Have stretched their yellow mimic stars
　And purple-banded sky;
The baby creeps beneath, perchance,
　And lying hidden there,
She clutches with her rosy hands
　The parti-colored square.

Here, with the gayly-knotted reel
  And spindle broke in twain,
The brown, dismantled spinning-wheel
  These fifty years has lain;
Where shall we find the stately dames,
  The noble maids and true,
Who stitched across the creaking frames
  Or spun the yarn of blue?

Ah! underneath the hanging eaves.
  The seamed and sloping roof.
A later spinner daily weaves
  A silken web and woof:
The watchful spider in and out
  Her empty wheel has fed,
And wound the distaff round about
  With silver-knotted thread.
  Dora Read Goodale, in " Wide Awake."

THE VOICE OF THE GRASS.

HERE I come creeping, creeping everywhere;
  By the dusty roadside,
  On the sunny hillside,
  Close by the noisy brook,
  In every shady nook,
I come creeping, creeping everywhere.

Here I come creeping, smiling everywhere;
  All round the open door,
  Where sit the aged poor;
  Here where the children play,
  In the bright and merry May,
I come creeping, creeping everywhere.

Here I come creeping, creeping everywhere;
  In the noisy city street
  My pleasant face you'll meet.
  Cheering the sick at heart
  Toiling his busy part.—
Silently creeping, creeping everywhere.

Here I come creeping, creeping everywhere;
    You cannot see me coming,
    Nor hear my low sweet humming;
    For in the starry night,
    And the glad morning light,
I come quietly creeping everywhere.

Here I come creeping, creeping everywhere;
    More welcome than the flowers
    In summer's pleasant hours;
    The gentle cow is glad,
    And the merry bird not sad,
To see me creeping, creeping everywhere.

Here I come creeping, creeping everywhere;
    When you're numbered with the dead
    In your still and narrow bed,
    In the happy spring I'll come
    And deck your silent home,—
Creeping, silently creeping everywhere.

Here I come creeping, creeping everywhere;
    My humble song of praise
    Most joyfully I raise
    To Him at whose command
    I beautify the land,
Creeping, silently creeping everywhere.
              Sarah Roberts.

THE DANDELIONS.

The sun shone into the garden,
    The children were all at play;
They gathered the dandelions,
    And threw them at little May.

She laughed when the yellow blossoms
    •Came falling around her head,
And, clapping her hands together,
    In wondering tones she said:

"Oh, sisters! the stars were shining
　　Last night in the dark, dark sky,
And mamma said God had set them
　　To light the poor travelers by.

"I'm sure that we do not need them
　　To shine for us in the day;
But here they are lying around us,
　　And lighting us while we play."

Then Emily stooped to kiss her,
　　And said, "No, my darling one,
These things are not stars, but flowers,
　　That open to greet the sun.

"They stare at him through the daytime,
　　And when he has gone to rest,
They close all their yellow petals,
　　And nestle to earth's warm breast.

"You see they are only flowers;"
　　But May shook her head in doubt:—
"I know they are stars, dear sister,
　　They're stars with the fire put out."
　　　　　　　　Amelia D. Alden.

GRANDMOTHER'S STORY OF BUNKER HILL BATTLE,

AS SHE SAW IT FROM THE BELFRY.

'TIS like stirring living embers, when, at eighty, one remembers
All the achings and the quakings of "the times that tried men's souls;"
When I talk of *Whig* and *Tory*, when I tell the *Rebel* story,
To you the words are ashes, but to me they're burning coals.

I had heard the muskets' rattle of the April
    running battle;
Lord Percy's hunted soldiers, I can see their
    red coats still;
But a deadly chill comes o'er me, as the day
    looms up before me,
When a thousand men lay bleeding on the
    slopes of Bunker Hill.

'Twas a peaceful summer's morning, when the
    first thing gave us warning
Was the booming of the cannon from the
    river and the shore;
"Child," says grandma, "what's the matter?
    what is all this noise and clatter?
Have those scalping Indian devils come to
    murder us once more?"

Poor old soul! my sides were shaking in the
    midst of all my quaking,
To hear her talk of Indians when the guns
    began to roar;
She had seen the burning village, and the
    slaughter and the pillage,
When the Mohawks killed her father with
    their bullets through the door.

Then I said, "Now, dear old granny, don't you
    fret and worry any,
For I'll soon come back and tell you whether
    this is work or play;
There can't be mischief in it, so I won't be
    gone a minute"—
For a minute then I started. I was gone the
    livelong day.

No time for bodice-lacing or for looking-glass
    grimacing;
Down my hair went as I hurried, tumbling
    half-way to my heels;

God forbid your ever knowing, when there's
   blood around her flowing,
How the lonely, helpless daughter of a quiet
   household feels!

In the street I heard a thumping; and I knew
   it was the stumping
Of the Corporal, our old neighbor, on that
   wooden leg he wore.
With a knot of women round him—it was
   lucky I had found him,
So I followed with the others, and the
   Corporal marched before.

They were making for the steeple,—the old
   soldier and his people;
The pigeons circled round us as we climbed
   the creaking stair.
Just across the narrow river—oh, so close it
   made me shiver!
Stood a fortress on the hill-top that but
   yesterday was bare.

Not slow our eyes to find it: well we knew
   who stood behind it,
Though the earth-work hid them from us, and
   the stubborn walls were dumb:
Here were sister, wife, and mother, looking
   wild upon each other,
And their lips were white with terror as they
   said, "THE HOUR HAS COME!"

The morning slowly wasted, not a morsel had
   we tasted,
And our heads were almost splitting with the
   cannon's deafening thrill,
When a figure tall and stately round the
   rampart strode sedately;
It was PRESCOTT, once since told me; he
   commanded on the hill.

Every woman's heart grew bigger when we
  saw his manly figure,
With the banyan buckled round it, standing
  up so straight and tall;
Like a gentleman of leisure who is strolling
  out for pleasure,
Through the storm of shells and cannon shot
  he walked around the wall.

At eleven the streets were swarming, for the
  red-coats' ranks were forming;
At noon in marching order they were moving
  to the piers;
How the bayonets gleamed and glistened, as
  we looked far down and listened
To the trampling and the drum beat of the
  belted grenadiers.

At length the men have started, with a cheer
  (it seemed faint-hearted),
In their scarlet regimentals, with their knap-
  sacks on their backs,
And the reddening, rippling water, as after a
  sea-fight's slaughter,
Round the barges gliding onward blushed like
  blood along their tracks.

So they crossed to the other border, and again
  they formed in order;
And the boats came back for soldiers, came
  for soldiers, soldiers still;
The time seemed everlasting to us women
  faint and fasting—
At last they're moving, marching, marching
  proudly up the hill.

We can see the bright steel glancing all along
  the lines advancing—
Now the front rank fires a volley— they have
  thrown away their shot;

For behind their earthwork lying, all the balls
above them flying,
Our people need not hurry; so they wait and
answer not.

Then the Corporal, our old cripple (he would
swear sometimes and tipple)—
He had heard the bullets whistle (in the old
French war) before—
Calls out in words of jeering, just as if they
were all hearing—
And his wooden leg thumps fiercely on the
dusty belfry floor:—

"Oh! fire away, ye villains, and earn King
George's shillin's,
But ye'll waste a ton of powder before a 'rebel'
falls:
You may bang the dirt and welcome, they're
as safe as Dan'l Malcolm
Ten feet beneath the gravestone that you've
splintered with your balls!"

In the hush of expectation, in the awe and
trepidation
Of the dread approaching moment, we are
well-nigh breathless all;
Though the rotten bars are failing on the
rickety belfry railing,
We are crowding up against them like the
waves against a wall.

Just a glimpse (the air is clearer), they are
nearer,—nearer,—nearer,
When a flash—a curling smoke-wreath—then
a crash—the steeple shakes
The deadly truce is ended: the tempest's
shroud is rended;
Like a morning mist it gathered, like a
thunder-cloud it breaks!

Oh the sight our eyes discover as the blue-
    black smoke blows over!
The red-coats stretched in windrows as a
    mower rakes his hay;
Here a scarlet heap is lying, there a headlong
    crowd is flying
Like a billow that has broken and is shivered
    into spray.

Then we cried, "The troops are routed! They
    are beat—it can't be doubted!
God be thanked, the fight is over!"—Ah! the
    grim old soldier's smile!
"Tell us, tell us why you look so!" (we could
    hardly speak, we shook so)
"Are they beaten? Are they beaten? ARE
    they beaten?" "Wait a while."

Oh the trembling and the terror! for too soon
    we saw our error:
They are baffled, not defeated; we have
    driven them back in vain;
And the columns that were scattered, round
    the colors that were tattered,
Toward the sullen silent fortress turn their
    belted breasts again.

All at once, as we are gazing, lo the roofs of
    Charlestown blazing!
They have fired the harmless village; in an
    hour it will be down!
The Lord in heaven confound them, rain his
    fire and brimstone round them,—
The robbing, murdering red-coats, that would
    burn a peaceful town!

They are marching, stern and solemn; we can
    see each massive column
As they near the naked earth-mound with the
    slanting walls so steep.

Have our soldiers got faint-hearted, and in
    noiseless haste departed?
Are they panic-struck and helpless? Are they
    palsied or asleep?

Now! the walls they're almost under! scarce a
    rod the foes asunder!
Not a firelock flashed against them! up the
    earthwork they will swarm!
But the words have scarce been spoken, when
    the ominous calm is broken,
And a bellowing crash has emptied all the
    vengeance of the storm!

Lo again, with murderous slaughter, pelted
    backwards to the water,
Fly Pigot's running heroes, and the frightened
    braves of Howe;
And we shout, "At last they're done for, it's
    their barges they have run for:
They are beaten, beaten, beaten; and the
    battle's over now!"

And we looked, poor timid creatures, on the
    rough old soldier's features,
Our lips afraid to question, but he knew what
    we would ask:
"Not sure," he said; "Keep quiet,—once
    more, I guess, they'll try it—
Here's damnation to the cut-throats!"—then
    he handed me his flask,

Saying, "Gal, you're looking shaky; have a
    drop of old Jamaiky;
I'm afraid there'll be more trouble afore the
    job is done;"
So I took one scorching swallow; dreadful
    faint I felt and hollow,
Standing there from early morning when the
    firing was begun.

All through those hours of trial I had watched
    a calm clock dial,
As the hands kept creeping, creeping,—they
    were creeping round to four,
When the old man said, "They're forming
    with their bayonets fixed for storming:
It's the death-grip that's a coming,—they will
    try the works once more."

With brazen trumpets blaring, the flames
    behind them glaring,
The deadly wall before them, in close array
    they come;
Still onward, upward toiling, like a dragon's
    fold uncoiling—
Like the rattlesnake's shrill warning the
    reverberating drum!

Over heaps all torn and gory—shall I tell the
    fearful story,
How they surged above the breastwork, as a
    sea breaks over a deck;
How driven, yet scarce defeated, our worn-
    out men retreated,
With their powder-horns all emptied, like the
    swimmers from a wreck?

It has all been told and painted; as for me
    they say I fainted,
And the wooden-legged old Corporal stumped
    with me down the stair.
And when I woke from dreams affrighted the
    evening lamps were lighted,—
On the floor a youth was lying; his bleeding
    breast was bare.

And I heard through all the flurry, "Send for
    Warren! hurry! hurry!
Tell him here's a soldier bleeding, and he'll
    come and dress his wound!"

Ah, we knew not till the morrow told its tale
of death and sorrow,
How the starlight found him stiffened on the
dark and bloody ground.

Who the youth was, what his name was,
where the place from which he came was,
Who had brought him from the battle, and
had left him at our door,
He could not speak to tell us; but 'twas one
of our brave fellows,
As the homespun plainly showed us which
the dying soldier wore.

For they all thought he was dying, as they
gathered round him crying,—
And they said, "Oh, how they'll miss him!"
and, "What *will* his mother do?"
Then, his eyelids just unclosing like a child's
that has been dozing,
He faintly murmured, "Mother!"—and—I
saw his eyes were blue.

"Why grandma, how you're winking!"—
"Ah, my child, it sets me thinking
Of a story not like this one. Well, he
somehow lived along:
So we came to know each other, and I nursed
him like a—mother,
'Till at last he stood before me, tall and
rosy-cheeked, and strong.

And we sometimes walked together in the
pleasant summer weather;
—"Please to tell us what his name was!"—
Just your own, my little dear,—
There's his picture Copley painted; we became
so well acquainted,
That—in short, that's why I'm grandma, and
you children all are here."
     Oliver Wendell Holmes.

THE INCHCAPE ROCK.

No stir in the air, no stir in the sea,—
The ship was still as she might be;
Her sails from heaven received no motion;
Her keel was steady in the ocean.

Without either sign or sound of their shock,
The waves flowed over the Inchcape rock;
So little they rose, so little they fell,
They did not move the Inchcape bell.

The holy abbot of Aberbrothok
Had floated that bell on the Inchcape rock:
On the waves of the storm it floated and swung,
And louder and louder its warning rung.

When the rock was hid by the tempest's swell,
The mariners heard the warning bell;
And then they knew the perilous rock
And blessed the priest of Aberbrothok.

The sun in heaven shone so gay,—
All things were joyful on that day;
The sea-birds screamed as they sported round,
And there was pleasure in their sound.

The float of the Inchcape bell was seen,
A darker speck on the ocean green;
Sir Ralph, the rover, walked his deck,
And he fixed his eyes on the darker speck.

He felt the cheering power of spring,—
It made him whistle, it made him sing;
His heart was mirthful to excess;
But the rover's mirth was wickedness.

His eye was on the bell and float,
Quoth he, "My men, pull out the boat;
And row me to the Inchcape rock,
And I'll plague the priest of Aberbrothok."

The boat is lowered, the boatmen row,
And to the Inchcape rock they go;
Sir Ralph bent over from the boat,
And cut the warning bell from the float.

Down sank the bell with a gurgling sound;
The bubbles rose, and burst around,
Quoth Sir Ralph, "The next who comes to the rock
Will not bless the priest of Aberbrothok."

Sir Ralph, the rover, sailed away,—
He scoured the seas for many a day;
And now, grown rich with plundered store,
He steers his course to Scotland's shore.

So thick a haze o'erspreads the sky
They could not see the sun on high;
The wind hath blown a gale all day;
At evening it hath died away.

On the deck the rover takes his stand;
So dark it is they see no land.
Quoth Sir Ralph, "It will be lighter soon,
For there is the dawn of the rising moon."

"Canst hear," said one, "the breakers roar?
For yonder, methinks should be the shore.
Now where we are I cannot tell,
But I wish we could hear the Inchcape bell."

They hear no sound; the swell is strong;
Though the wind hath fallen, they drift along;
Till the vessel strikes with a shivering shock,—
Alas! it is the Inchcape rock!

Sir Ralph, the rover, tore his hair
He beat himself in wild despair.
The waves rush in on every side;
The ship is sinking beneath the tide.

But ever in his dying fear
One dreadful sound he seemed to hear,—
A sound as if with the Inchcape bell
The evil spirit was ringing his knell.

Robert Southey.

THE HUMBLE-BEE.

Burly, dozing humble-bee,
Where thou art is clime for me.
Let them sail for Porto Rique,
Far-off heats through seas to seek;
I will follow thee alone,
Thou animated torrid-zone!
Zigzag steerer, desert cheerer,
Let me chase thy waving lines;
Keep me nearer, me thy hearer,
Singing over shrubs and vines.

Insect lover of the sun,
Joy of thy dominion!
Sailor of the atmosphere;
Swimmer through the waves of air;
Voyager of light and noon·
Epicurean of June;
Wait, I prithee, till I come
Within earshot of thy hum,—
All without is martyrdom.

When the south wind, in May days,
With a net of shining haze
Silver the horizon wall,
And with softness touching all,
Tints the human countenance
With a color of romance,
And infusing subtle heats,
Turns the sod to violets,

Thou in sunny solitudes,
Rover of the underwoods,
The green silence dost displace
With thy mellow, breezy bass.

Hot mid-summer's petted crone,
Sweet to me thy drowsy tone
Tells of countless sunny hours,
Long days, and solid banks of flowers;
Of gulfs of sweetness without bound
In Indian wildernesses found;
Of Syrian peace, immortal leisure,
Firmest cheer, and bird-like pleasure.

Aught unsavory or unclean
Hath my insect never seen;
But violets and bilberry bells,
Maple-sap and daffodels,
Grass with green flag half-mast high,
Succory to match the sky,
Columbine with horn of honey,
Scented fern, and agrimony,
Clover, catchfly, adder's-tongue
And brier-roses, dwelt among;
All beside was unknown waste,
All was picture as he passed.

Wiser far than human seer,
Yellow-breeched philosopher!
Seeing only what is fair,
Sipping only what is sweet,
Thou dost mock at fate and care,
Leave the chaff, and take the wheat.
When the fierce northwestern blast
Cools sea and land so far and fast,
Thou already slumberest deep;
Woe and want thou canst outsleep,
Want and woe which torture us,
Thy sleep makes ridiculous.
                    Ralph Waldo Emerson.

BRUCE AND THE SPIDER.

For Scotland's and for freedom's right
   The Bruce his part had played,
In five successive fields of fight
   Been conquered and dismayed;
Once more against the English host
His band he led and once more lost
   The meed for which he fought;
And now from battle, faint and worn,
The homeless fugitive forlorn
   A hut's lone shelter sought.

And cheerless was that resting-place
   For him who claimed a throne;
His canopy, devoid of grace,
   The rude, rough beams alone;
The heather couch his only bed,—
Yet well I ween had slumber fled
   From couch of eider-down!
Through darksome night till dawn of day,
Absorbed in wakeful thought he lay
   Of Scotland and her crown.

The sun rose brightly, and its gleam
   Fell on that hapless bed,
And tinged with light each shapeless beam
   Which roofed the lowly shed;
When, looking up with wistful eye,
The Bruce beheld a spider try
   His filmy thread to fling
From beam to beam of that rude cot;
And well the insect's toilsome lot
   Taught Scotland's future king.

Six times his gossamery thread
   The wary spider threw;
In vain the filmy line was sped,
   For powerless or untrue

Each aim appeared, and back recoiled
The patient insect, six times foiled,
   And yet unconquered still:
And soon the Bruce, with eager eye,
Saw him prepare once more to try
   His courage, strength, and skill.

One effort more, his seventh and last!
   The hero hailed the sign!
And on the wished-for beam hung fast
   That slender silken line;
Slight as it was, his spirit caught
The more than omen, for his thought
   The lesson well could trace,
Which even "he who runs may read,"
That Perseverence gains its meed,
   And Patience wins the race.
               Bernard Barton.

TO A WATERFOWL.

WHITHER, midst falling dew
While glow the heavens with the last steps
   of day,
Far, through their rosy depths, dost thou
   pursue
   Thy solitary way?

Vainly the fowler's eye
Might mark thy distant flight to do the wrong,
As, darkly seen against the crimson sky,
   Thy figure floats along.

Seek'st thou the plashy brink
Of weedy lake, or marge of river wide,
Or where the rocking billows rise and sink
   On the chafed ocean side?

There is a Power whose care
Teaches thy way along that pathless coast,—
The desert and illimitable air
   Lone wandering, but not lost.

All day thy wings have fanned,
At that far height, the cold, thin atmosphere,
Yet stoop not, weary, to the welcome land,
   Though the dark night is near.

And soon that toil shall end;
Soon shalt thou find a summer home, and rest,
And scream among thy fellows; reeds shall
      bend,
   Soon, o'er thy sheltered nest.

Thou'rt gone, the abyss of heaven
Hath swallowed up thy form; yet, on my
      heart
Deeply hath sunk the lesson thou hast given,
   And shall not soon depart:

He who, from zone to zone,
Guides through the boundless sky thy certain
      flight,
In the long way that I must tread alone,
   Will lead my steps aright.
                     Wm. Cullen Bryant.

BABY'S SKIES.

Would you know the baby's skies?
Baby's skies are mother's eyes.
Mother's eyes and smile together
Make the baby's pleasant weather.

Mother, keep your eyes from tears,
Keep your heart from foolish fears,
Keep your lips from dull complaining
Lest the baby think 'tis raining.
              M. C. Bartlett.

WHO STOLE THE BIRD'S NEST?

"To WHIT! to whit! to whee!
Will you listen to me?
Who stole four eggs I laid,
And the nice, warm nest I made?"

"Not I," said the cow—"moo-oo!
Such a thing I'd never do.
I gave you a wisp of hay,
But did not take your nest away.
Not I," said the cow—"moo-oo!
Such a thing I'd never do."

"Bobolink! bobolink!
Now, what do you think?
Who stole a nest away
From the plum-tree to-day?"

"Not I," said the dog—"bow-wow!
I couldn't be so mean, I trow.
I gave hairs, the nest to make,
But the nest I didn't take.
Not I," said the dog—"bow-wow!
I couldn't be so mean, I trow."

"Bobolink! bobolink!
Now, what do you think?
Who stole a nest away
From the plum-tree to-day?"

"Cuckoo! cuckoo! cuckoo!
Let me speak a word, too.
Who stole that pretty nest
From poor little yellow-breast?"

"Baa! baa!" said the sheep—"oh, no!
I wouldn't treat a poor bird so.
I gave wool, the nest to line,

But the nest was none of mine.
Baa! baa!" said the sheep—"oh, no!
I wouldn't treat a poor bird so."

"To whit! to whit! to whee!
Will you listen to me?
Who stole four eggs I laid,
And the nice, warm nest I made?"

"Bobolink! bobolink!
Now, what do you think?
Who stole a nest away
From the plum-tree to-day?"

"Cuckoo! cuckoo! cuckoo!
Let me speak a word, too.
Who stole that pretty nest
From poor little yellow-breast?"

"Caw! caw!" said the crow,
"I should like to know
What thief took away
A bird's nest to-day!"

"Cluck! cluck!" said the hen—
"Don't ask me again.
Why, I haven't a chick
That would do such a trick!

"We all gave her a feather,
And she wove them together.
I'd scorn to intrude
On her and her brood.
Cluck! cluck!" said the hen—
"Don't ask me again."

"Chira whirr! chira whirr!
Let us make a great stir;
Let us find out his name,
And all cry—'for shame!'"

"I would not rob a bird,"
Said little Mary Green;
"I think I never heard
Of anything so mean."

"It's very cruel, too!"
Said little Alice Neal;
"I wonder if he knew
How bad the bird would feel!"

A little boy hung down his head,
And went and hid behind the bed,
For *he* stole that pretty nest
From poor little yellow-breast,
And he felt so full of shame,
He didn't like to tell his name.
      Mrs. L. M. Child.

THE CAT'S DINNER-TIME.

LOTH at once to leave her play
 Under the pear-tree, Bessie stands:
"Mamma, why do you always say
 'Come to dinner, and wash your hands?'
There's my kitty—you said to-day
 You only wished I were half as neat—
She don't bother herself to stay
 And wash her hands when she wants to eat.

"*After* dinner I've seen her sit
 And wash herself for an hour or more,
And smooth her kitten, and tidy it—
 She never does it at all *before.*"
Mamma laughed. "There was once a time,
 Ages and ages long ago,
When mice could reason, and birds make rhyme,
 And cats could talk—or they tell us so.

"Then all cathood (or so 'tis writ
I read it once in a book of mine),
Grown-up tabby and little kit,
  Washed their hands when they went to dine.
Once, a cat of an ancient house,
  Mindful always of social laws,
Caught a frightened and trembling mouse,
  And as she held him with teeth and claws,

" 'O,' said he, 'you're forgetting quite
  What even a poor mouse understands—
It isn't tidy, nor yet polite
  To eat before you have washed your hands!'
So a moment the cat put by
  Her longed-for dinner, to wash herself,
And—whisk!—he found, without one good-by,
  The mouse-hole under the pantry shelf!

" 'There!' said the cat, with a vexed grimace,
  'Hereafter, whether in field or town,
I never will wash my hands and face,
  Until my dinner is safely down!'
And ever since, it is said, my sweet,
  All the kittens beneath the sun,
Rush unwashed when they're called to eat,
  And make their toilet when dinner's done!"
    Elizabeth Akers Allen, in " Our Little
      Men and Women."

TO MOTHER FAIRIE.

GOOD old mother Fairie,
  Sitting by your fire,
Have you any little folk
  You would like to hire?

I want no chubby drudges
  To milk and churn and spin,
Nor old and wrinkled Brownies,
  With grisly beards and thin:

But patient little people,
  With hands of busy care,
And gentle speech and loving hearts;
  Say, have you such to spare?

I know a poor pale body,
  Who cannot sleep at night,
And I want the little people
  To keep her chamber bright:

To chase away the shadows
  That make her moan and weep,
To sing her loving lullabies,
  And kiss her eyes asleep.

And when in dreams she reaches
  For pleasures dead and gone,
To hold her wasted fingers,
  And make her rings stay on.

They must be very cunning
  To make the future shine
Like leaves, and flowers, and strawberries,
  A-growing on one vine.

Good old mother Fairie,
  Since my need you know,
Tell me, have you any folk
  Wise enough to go?
            Alice Cary.

THE GLADNESS OF NATURE.

Is THIS a time to be cloudy and sad,
  When our mother Nature laughs around;
When even the deep blue heavens look glad,
  And gladness breathes from the blossoming ground?

There are notes of joy from the hang-bird and
    wren,
  And the gossip of swallows through all the
    sky;
The ground-squirrel gayly chirps by his den,
And the wilding bee hums merrily by.

The clouds are at play in the azure space
  And their shadows at play on the bright-
    green vale,
And here they stretch to the frolic chase,
  And there they roll on the easy gale.

There's a dance of leaves in that aspen bower,
  There's a titter of winds in that beechen tree.
There's a smile on the fruit, and a smile on
    the flower,
  And a laugh from the brook that runs to
    the sea.

And look at the broad-faced sun, how he
    smiles
On the dewy earth that smiles in his ray,
On the leaping waters and gay young isles;
  Ay, look, and he'll smile thy gloom away.
              Wm. Cullen Bryant.

SUPPOSE!

Suppose, my little lady,
  Your doll should break her head,
Could you make it whole by crying
  Till your eyes and nose are red?
And would n't it be pleasanter
  To treat it as a joke:
And say you're glad " 'Twas Dolly's
  And not your head that broke?"

Suppose you're dressed for walking.
  And the rain comes pouring down.
Will it clear off any sooner
  Because you scold and frown?

And would n't it be nicer
  For you to smile than pout,
And so make sunshine in the house
  Where there is none without?

Suppose your task, my little man,
  Is very hard to get,
Will it make it any easier
  For you to sit and fret?
And would n't it be wiser
  Than waiting like a dunce,
To go to work in earnest
  And learn the thing at once?

Suppose that some boys have a horse,
  And some a coach and pair,
Will it tire you less while walking
  To say, "It is n't fair?"
And would n't it be nobler
  To keep your temper sweet,
And in your heart be thankful
  You can walk upon your feet?

And suppose the world do n't please you,
  Nor the way some people do,
Do you think the whole creation
  Will be altered just for you?
And is n't it, my boy or girl,
  The wisest, bravest plan,
Whatever comes, or does n't come,
  To do the best you can?
                        Phœbe Cary.

AN INCIDENT OF THE FIRE AT HAMBURG.

THE tower of old Saint Nicholas soared
  upward to the skies,
Like some huge piece of Nature's make, the
  growth of centuries;

You could not deem its crowding spires a
    work of human art,
They seemed to struggle lightward from a
    sturdy living heart.

Not Nature's self more freely speaks in crystal
    or in oak,
Than, through the pious builder's hand, in
    that gray pile she spoke;
And as from acorn springs the oak, so, freely
    and alone,
Sprang from his heart this hymn to God, sung
    in obedient stone.

It seemed a wondrous freak of chance, so
    perfect, yet so rough,
A whim of Nature crystallized slowly in
    granite tough;
The thick spires yearned towards the sky in
    quaint, harmonious lines,
And in broad sunlight basked and slept, like
    a grove of blasted pines.

Never did rock or stream or tree lay claim
    with better right
To all the adorning sympathies of shadow and
    of light;
And, in that forest petrified, as forester there
    dwells
Stout Herman, the old sacristan, sole lord of
    all its bells.

Surge leaping after surge, the fire roared
    onward red as blood,
Till half of Hamburg lay engulfed beneath the
    eddying flood;
For miles away, the fiery spray poured down
    its deadly rain,
And back and forth the billows sucked, and
    paused, and burst again.

From square to square with tiger leaps rushed
   on the lustful fire,
The air to leeward shuddered with the gasps
   of its desire;
And church and palace, which even now
   stood whelmed but to the knee,
Lift their black roofs like breakers lone amid
   the whirling sea.

Up in his tower old Herman sat and watched
   with quiet look;
His soul had trusted God too long to be at
   last forsook;
He could not fear, for surely God a pathway
   would unfold
Through this red sea for faithful hearts, as
   once he did of old.

But scarcely can he cross himself, or on his
   good saint call,
Before the sacrilegious flood o'erleaped the
   church-yard wall;
And ere a *pater* half was said, 'mid smoke
   and crackling glare,
His island tower scarce juts its head above
   the wide despair.

Upon the peril's desperate peak his heart
   stood up sublime;
His first thought was for God above, his next
   was for his chime;
"Sing now, and make your voices heard in
   hymns of praise," cried he,
"As did the Israelites of old, safe walking
   through the sea!

"Through this red sea our God hath made the
   pathway safe to shore;
Our promised land stands full in sight; shout
   now as ne'er before!"

And as the tower came crushing down, the
  bells, in clear accord,
Pealed forth the grand old German hymn,—
  "All good souls, praise the Lord!"

James Russell Lowell.

LANDING OF THE PILGRIM FATHERS.

THE breaking waves dashed high
  On a stern and rock-bound coast,
And the woods against a stormy sky
  Their giant branches tossed;

And the heavy night hung dark
  The hills and waters o'er,
When a band of exiles moored their bark
  On the wild New England shore.

Not as the conqueror comes,
  They the true-hearted, came;
Not with the roll of stirring drums,
  And the trumpet that sings of fame;

Not as the flying come,
  In silence and in fear,—
They shook the depths of the desert's gloom
  With their hymns of lofty cheer.

Amidst the storm they sang,
  And the stars heard and the sea!
And the sounding aisles of the dim wood rang
  To the anthems of the free!

The ocean-eagle soared
  From his nest by the white wave's foam,
And the rocking pines of the forest roared,—
  This was their welcome home!

There were men with hoary hair
  Amidst that pilgrim-band;—
Why had they come to wither there,
  Away from their childhood's land?

There was woman's fearless eye,
　Lit by her deep love's truth;
There was manhood's brow serenely high,
　And the fiery heart of youth.

What sought they thus afar?
　Bright jewels of the mine?
The wealth of seas, the spoils of war?—
　They sought a faith's pure shrine!

Ay, call it holy ground,
　The soil where first they trod!
They left unstained what there they found,—
　Freedom to worship God.
　　　　　　　　Felicia Hemans.

TO THE LADY-BIRD.

LADY-BIRD! lady-bird! fly away home,—
　The field-mouse is gone to her nest,
The daisies have shut up their sleepy red eyes,
　And the bees and the birds are at rest.

Lady-bird! lady-bird! fly away home,—
　The glow-worm is lighting her lamp,
The dew's falling fast, and your fine speckled
　　wings
Will flag with the close-clinging damp.

Lady-bird! lady-bird! fly away home,—
　The fairy bells tinkle afar!
Make haste, or they'll catch ye, and harness
　　ye fast
With a cobweb to Oberon's car.

Lady-bird! lady-bird! fly away home,—
　To your house in the old willow-tree,
Where your children, so dear, have invited
　　the ant
And a few cozy neighbors to tea.

Lady-bird! lady-bird! fly away home,—
And, if not gobbled up by the way,
Nor yoked by the fairies to Oberon's car,
You're in luck,—and that's all I've to say.
Mrs. Southey.

THE SEASON THAT IS COMING.

SWEET, sweet, sweet is the season that is coming;
Sweet the wayside wild rose and the wild bee's humming;
Sweet the pink azalia in the woods' recesses,
Sweet the nodding barberry buds, wearing yellow dresses,
Sweet the scarlet columbine climbing up the ledges,
Sweet the pale anemone in the forest edges,
Sweet the rosy apple blooms, sweet the birds among them,
Sweet the petals in the grass where the winds have flung them.

Sweet, sweet, sweet are the gardens overflowing
With pinks and yellow marigolds, and mignonette a-blowing,
With four-o'clocks and London-pride, and pretty pansy faces,
With honeysuckle by the wall, and roses in all places;
And sweet the happy children who come from days of duty
To find the fair earth all a-bloom, a place of perfect beauty
Books thrown away, they laugh and play, with sun and sweet winds blowing,
A rose blooms out on every cheek, and pinks in the lips are growing.

Sweet the breeze-blown pastures with violets
running over;
Sweet the meadows stretching wide crowded
with white clover;
Sweet the thickets starred with flowers and
flushed with growing berries.
And pretty dinners set for birds of rose-hips
and wild cherries;
Sweet the corners dim and deep where
floating boughs are meeting.
And little lovers come and go with songs of
happy greeting;
Sweet the fronds of fairy fern in hidden nooks
unfolding;
Sweet the thoughts in loving hearts these
lovely things beholding.
   Mrs. M. F. Butts, in "Wide Awake."

QUEEN MABEL.

"GREEN, green are the meadows,
 And blue, blue is the sky,
 And glad, glad is the morning,
 And happy and gay am I.
Tirra-la-la, la, la, la !
 And happy and gay am I.

"White, white are the daisies
 Blossoming everywhere,
 And red, red are the roses,
 And sweet, sweet is the air!

"And sweet is the burnie's music,
 And the music of bee and bird
Ha, ha! the sweetest music
 That ever and ever you heard!

"Gold, golden the sunbeams,
 And bright, bright is the day,
 And the bees, and the birds, and Mabel,
 Little of care have they!

"Oh! and over the meadows,
　Oh! and under the sky,
And all in the dewy morning,
　Happy and gay am I'
Tirra-la-la, la, la, la!
　Happy and gay am I!

The queen passed by in her carriage,
　And little Mabel's song,
By a roving zephyr wafted.
　She heard as she rode along.
"Ah, child!" she sighed as she listened,
　A shadow upon her brow—
"With the birds, and the bees, and the
　　blossoms
　How happy and gay art thou!"

Standing knee-deep in clover,
　Mabel looked up and saw
The glitter and royal splendor,
　And her voice was hushed with awe;
And the light from her sweet eyes faded,
　And the song died out of her heart;
"O queen!" she sighed in her envy,
　"How happy and grand thou art!"

And the glee was gone from the morning,
　The gladness gone from the day,
As through the tangle of clover
　She wearily took her way.
"What a wretched place to live in!"
　She paused at a cottage door.
"How lowly and plain and humble!
　I never noticed before!"
And over her work she muttered,
　"Little the queen of the land
With the soot and grime of the kitchen
　Needs ever to soil her hand!"
And over her simple sewing,
　As the afternoon went by,
Often she fell to musing,

Often she breathed a sigh;
  And often she thus would murmur—
"I doubt if ever the queen
  Would deign, with the jeweled fingers,
To sew an inch of a seam."
  And wearily on her pillow
    At even she laid her head;
"I never shall be a queen," she sobbed,
  "And I wish that I were dead!"

But presently came a message,
  Reading—oh, was it true?—
"Arise and come to me, Mabel;
  I, the queen, have sent for you."
Then quick to the royal palace
  She rode in the carriage grand,
And they led her through halls of marble
  To the queen of all the land;
And the queen arose, and laying
  Her crown at Mabel's feet,
"I go to be free and happy,
  And play in the meadows sweet,"
She said, and to all her people—
  "Farewell!" and "farewell!" she said;
And the people took up the golden crown
  And put it on Mabel's head.
And oh! it was heavy, heavy!
  Heavy, heavy as lead!

To a gilded throne they brought her,
  In purple and ermine clad.
"Hail to thee, fair queen Mabel!"
  They shouted with voices glad;
And "Hail to thee, fair queen Mabel!"
  Rang in her ears all day,
Till, weary, herself she questioned
  "Is it right, is it right to stay?
To drive the cows from the pasture
  Is Mabel's task alone;
And my father at work since morning,
  He will soon be coming home.

"He will miss his little Mabel,
   For there is no one but me
To toast the bread for his supper
   And make him a cup of tea.
But no! am I not a lady?
   It is no care of mine
To worry about the supper
   And the milking of the kine!"

So she dwelt in the marble palace,
   And dined from a golden plate,
And slept in a silken chamber,
   And sat in the chair of state.
And whenever she went riding
   The people with cheers would greet,
And maidens and little children
   With blossoms would strew the street.

And royally thus lived Mable,
   Her only task—to command;
Servants, unnumbered, ready
   To move at the wave of her hand;
And alway about her lingered
   Gay courtiers, a dazzling throng;
And the blithe hours swiftly flitted
   With story and dance and song.
But often herself she questioned,
   As she sat on the gilded throne,
"How is it with them, I wonder—
   How is it with them at home?"

As the palace with mirth and music
   Echoed and rang, one night,
The people peered through the windows,
   Watching the festive sight:
And a beggar in rags and tatters,
   Listening, shook his fist;
"What right have they to be merry
   When my little ones starve?" he hissed.
And the people his words repeated:
   "What right, to be sure?" they said,

"Flaunting in silk and diamonds
  While our little ones cry for bread."

And ever, as thus they murmured,
  Louder their voices grew,
Till, all in a red-hot anger,
  To the palace doors they flew.
And the sentinels, at each entrance,
  Quickly they put to flight,
And hurried with cries and clamor
  Into the halls so bright—
Into the halls of marble,
  With clubs and with axes armed,
Till the sound of their shouts and curses
  The courtiers hearing, alarmed,
Fled in their silks and diamonds,
  Leaving the queen alone.
On rushed the riotous rabble,
  Making its way to the throne,
And they who had "Hail Queen Mabel!"
  Shouted with loyal will,
Now aloft their cruel weapons
  Brandished, intent to kill.

Then she shrieked for help in her terror,
  Never a friend came nigh.
So, as the crowd drew nearer,
  Sudden she turned to fly;
And casting aside the purple robe
  And the heavy golden crown,
Away and away she hastened,
  To the meadows she wandered down;
Down to the meadows wandered,
  Hastened away and away,
Till the birds and the dewy blossoms
  Were roused by the dawning day.

But the world it was sad and silent,
  Clouded and gray the morn,
As wearily on she wandered,
  Wearily and forlorn.

The burnie it went complaining,
　Fretting its way along,
Making no pleasant music,
　Singing no pleasant song;
And ever as in the hedges
　She came to a sweet wild rose,
At the touch of her queenly fingers
　The petals would sadly close.
Once did she call, "Sing, birdies!"
　But the little birds were dumb:
"Come to me as you used to!"
　But they, fearing, would not come.

"What a cozy place to live in!"
　She paused at a cottage door.
"Not a palace half so lovely
　Is there the country o'er!"
Within sat a woman knitting—
　A women aged and blind;
And ever she dropped the stitches,
　Trying in vain to find.
"Grandmother, let me help thee,"
　Mabel held out her hand.
"Nay," said the gray-haired woman,
　"Thou art the queen of the land!"

Just at that moment entered
　A workingman—quick she cried
"Father, oh, dost thou know me?"
　Sorrowfully he sighed,
"Oh, queen and gracious lady,
　Tell me if thou dost know
Aught of our little Mabel,
　Who was lost long years ago?
On a sunny summer morning
　She strayed from the meadows green,
Tell me if thou hast seen her—
　Tell me, oh, gracious queen!"

"Alas, they too have forgotten!"
　Bowing her head, she wept—

And the weeping queen awakened,
    And found she had only slept.
Safe in her low-ceiled chamber,
    Flooded with rosy light.
Only the little Mabel,
    The Mabel of yesternight!
Then aloud rejoicing sang she
    The song of the day gone by
"Glad, glad is the morning,
    And happy and gay am I!"
            Ellen Tracy Alden.

THEY DIDN'T THINK.

ONCE a trap was baited
    With a piece of cheese;
It tickled so a little mouse
    It almost made him sneeze;
An old rat said, "There's danger,
    Be careful where you go!"
"Nonsense!" said the other,
    "I don't think you know!"
So he walked in boldly—
    Nobody in sight;
First he took a nibble,
    Then he took a bite;
Close the trap together
    Snapped as quick as wink,
Catching mousey fast there,
    'Cause he didn't think.

Once a little turkey,
    Fond of her own way,
Wouldn't ask the old ones
    Where to go or stay;
She said, "I'm not a baby,

Here I am half-grown;
　Surely I am big enough
　To run about alone!"
Off she went, but somebody
　Hiding saw her pass;
Soon like snow her feathers
　Covered all the grass.
So she made a supper
　For a sly young mink,
'Cause she was so headstrong
　That she wouldn't think.

Once there was a robin
　Lived outside the door
Who wanted to go inside
　And hop upon the floor.
"No, no," said the mother,
　"You must stay with me;
Little birds are safest
　Sitting in a tree."
"I do n't care," said robin,
　And gave his tail a fling,
"I don't think the old folks
　Know quite everything."
Down he flew, and kitty seized him
　Before he'd time to blink
"Oh," he cried, "I'm sorry,
　But I didn't think."

Now my little children,
　You who read this song,
Don't you see what trouble
　Comes of thinking wrong?
And can't you take a warning
　From their dreadful fate
Who began their thinking
　When it was too late?
Don't think there's always safety
　Where no danger shows,
Don't suppose you know more

Than anybody knows;
But when you're warned of ruin.
Pause upon the brink.
And don't go under headlong.
'Cause you didn't think.
Phœbe Cary.

A MYSTERY.

Come children, and hear of the wizard Crum
  Crust:
In his magical box is some wonderful dust,
But keep the great secret, and mind each
  dark rule,
Perhaps you may see it before you leave
  school.
This dust is of diamonds with glittering
  grains
Of fine gold, and gems from the earth's
  deepest veins,
With parts of each insect, and flower, and
  tree,
And pearls from the depths of the tropical
  sea;
And fragments are there which a likeness
  reveal
To all that you fancy and all that you feel;
But this is most strange. if you use it with
  skill,
Great palaces rise, like Aladdin's, at will.
It wafts you to isles where the cocoa palms
  grow,
Or lands you 'mid icebergs, and darkness, and
  snow.
With might, if 'tis used, men may spring up
  in arms,
'Mid war's lurid gleamings. and cannon
  alarms;

Or melt into pity and charity too,
When sorrow's poor children it brings to their
 view.
It's traveling carpets are tables well spread
With this dust. There are mirrors of nations
 long dead,
And beautiful visions of gardens of bliss,
And life in a world that is better than this.

"Ha! ha! we have guessed it!" they cried
 with a shout.
"'Tis letters and books you are talking about."
"Well, well," he replied, "you have guessed
 very near;
My box is the great dictionary just here,
And magical, powerful, sharper than swords,
Are wonderful, terrible, beautiful WORDS."
Reaf Coral.

THE SECRET.

WE have a secret, just we three,—
The robin, and I, and the sweet cherry-tree;
The bird told the tree, and the tree told me,
And nobody knows it but just us three!

But of course the robin knows it best,
Because he built the—I shan't tell the rest!
And laid the four little—*somethings* in it;
—I am afraid I shall tell it every minute!

But if the tree and the robin don't peep,
I'll try my best the secret to keep;
Though I know when the little birds fly about,
Then the whole secret will be out!
Mrs. F. L. Ballard,
in " Youth's Companion.'

THE COMMON QUESTION.

BEHIND us at our evening meal
  The gray bird ate his fill,
Swung downward by a single claw,
  And wiped his hooked bill.

He shook his wings and crimson tail,
  And set his head aslant,
And, in his sharp, impatient way,
  Asked, "What does Charlie want?"

"Fie, silly bird!" I answered, "tuck
  Your head beneath your wing,
And go to sleep;"—but o'er and o'er
  He asked the selfsame thing.

Then, smiling, to myself I said:—
  How like are men and birds!
We all are saying what he says,
  In action or in words.

The boy with whip and top and drum,
  The girl with hoop and doll,
And men with lands and houses, ask
  The question of Poor Poll.

However full, with something more
  We fain the bag would cram;
We sigh above our crowded nets
  For fish that never swam.

No bounty of indulgent Heaven
  The vague desire can stay;
Self-love is still a Tartar mill
  For grinding prayers alway.

The dear God hears and pities all;
  He knoweth all our wants;
And what we blindly ask of him
  His love withholds or grants.

And so I sometimes think our prayers
  Might well be merged in one;
And nest and perch and hearth and church
  Repeat, " Thy will be done."
John Greenleaf Whittier.

FABLE.

THE mountain and the squirrel
Had a quarrel,
And the former called the latter
  " Little Prig;"
Bun replied,
"You are doubtless very big;
But all sorts of things and weather
Must be taken in together,
To make up a year
And a sphere.
And I think it no disgrace
To occupy my place.
If I'm not so large as you,
You are not so small as I,
And not half so spry.
I'll not deny you make
A very pretty squirrel track;
Talents differ; all is well and wisely put;
If I cannot carry forests on my back,
Neither can you crack a nut."
Ralph Waldo Emerson.

BABY.

Where did you come from, baby dear?
Out of the everywhere into here.

Where did you get your eyes so blue?
Out of the sky as I came through.

What makes the light in them sparkle and
   spin?
Some of the starry spikes left in.

Where did you get that little tear?
I found it waiting when I got here.

What makes your forehead so smooth and
   high?
A soft hand stroked it as I went by.

What makes your cheek like a warm white
   rose?
I saw something better than any one knows.

Whence that three-cornered smile of bliss?
Three angels gave me at once a kiss.

Where did you get this pearly ear?
God spoke, and it came out to hear.

Where did you get those arms and hands?
Love made itself into hooks and bands.

Feet, whence did you come, you darling
   things?
From the same box as the cherubs' wings.

How did they all just come to be you?
God thought about me, and so I grew.

But how did you come to us, you dear?
God thought about you, and so I am here.
George MacDonald.

ROBERT OF LINCOLN.

MERRILY swinging on briar and weed,
　Near to the nest of his little dame;
Over the mountain-side or mead,
　Robert of Lincoln is telling his name;
　　Bob-o-link, bob-o-link,
　　Spink, spank, spink;
Snug and safe is that nest of ours,
Hidden among the summer flowers.
　　Chee, chee, chee.

Robert of Lincoln is gaily dressed,
　Wearing a bright black wedding-coat;
White are his shoulders and white his crest,
　Hear him call in his merry note:
　　Bob-o-link, bob-o-link,
　　Spink, spank, spink;
Look what a nice new coat is mine,
Sure there was never a bird so fine.
　　Chee, chee, chee.

Robert of Lincoln's Quaker wife,
　Pretty and quiet, with plain brown wings,
Passing at home a patient life,
　Broods in the grass while her husband sings;
　　Bob-o-link, bob-o-link,
　　Spink, spank, spink;
Brood kind creature; you need not fear
Thieves and robbers while I am here.
　　Chee, chee, chee.

Modest and shy as a nun is she,
　One weak chirp is her only note,
Braggart, and prince of braggarts is he,

Pouring boasts from his little throat:
Bob-o-link, bob-o-link,
Spink, spank, spink:
Never was I afraid of man;
Catch me, cowardly knaves, if you can.
Chee, chee, chee.

Six white eggs on a bed of hay,
Flecked with purple, a pretty sight!
There as the mother sits all day,
Robert is singing with all his might;
Bob-o-link, bob-o-link,
Spink, spank, spink;
Nice, good wife, that never goes out,
Keeping house while I frolic about.
Chee, chee, chee.

Soon as the little ones chip the shell
Six wide mouths are open for food;
Robert of Lincoln bestirs him well,
Gathering seeds for the hungry brood.
Bob-o-link, bob-o-link,
Spink, spank, spink;
This new life is likely to be
Hard for a gay young fellow like me.
Chee, chee, chee.

Robert of Lincoln at length is made
Sober with work, and silent with care;
Off is his holiday garment laid,
Half forgotten that merry air,
Bob-o-link, bob-o-link,
Spink, spank, spink;
Nobody knows but my mate and I
Where our nest and our nestlings lie.
Chee, chee, chee.

Summer wanes; the children are grown;
Fun and frolic no more he knows;
Robert of Lincoln's a humdrum crone;

Off he flies, and we sing as he goes:
  Bob-o-link, bob-o-link,
  Spink, spank, spink;
When you can pipe that merry old strain,
Robert of Lincoln, come back again.
  Chee, chee, chee.
        William Cullen Bryant.

SMALL BEGINNINGS.

A TRAVELLER through a dusty road strewed acorns on the lea;
And one took root and sprouted up, and grew into a tree.
Love sought its shade, at evening time, to breathe its early vows;
And age was pleased, in heats of noon, to bask beneath its boughs;
The dormouse loved its dangling twigs, the birds sweet music bore;
It stood a glory in its place, a blessing evermore.

A little spring had lost its way amid the grass and fern,
A passing stranger scooped a well, where weary men might turn;
He walled it in, and hung with care a ladle at the brink;
He thought not of the deed he did, but judged that toil might drink.
He passed again, and lo! the well, by summers never dried,
Had cooled ten thousand parching tongues and saved a life beside.

A dreamer dropped a random thought, 't was
  old, and yet 't was new;
A simple fancy of the brain, but strong in
  being true.
It shone upon a genial mind, and lo! its light
  became
A lamp of life, a beacon ray, a monitory
  flame.
The thought was small; its issues great; a
  watchfire on a hill;
It sheds its radiance far adown, and cheers
  the valley still!

A nameless man, amid a crowd that thronged
  the daily mart,
Let fall a word of Hope and Love unstudied
  from the heart;
A whisper on the tumult thrown,—a transi-
  tory breath,—
It raised a brother from the dust; it saved a
  soul from death.
O germ! O fount! O word of love! O thought
  at random cast!
Ye were but little at the first, but mighty at
  the last.
Charles Mackay.

A PSALM OF LIFE.

TELL me not, in mournful numbers,
  "Life is but an empty dream!"
For the soul is dead that slumbers,
  And things are not what they seem.

Life is real! Life is earnest!
  And the grave is not its goal;
"Dust thou art, to dust returnest,"
  Was not spoken of the soul.

Not enjoyment, and not sorrow,
　Is our destined end or way:
But to act, that each to-morrow
　Find us farther than to-day.

Art is long, and Time is fleeting,
　And our hearts, though stout and brave,
Still, like muffled drums, are beating
　Funeral marches to the grave.

In the world's broad field of battle,
　In the bivouac of Life,
Be not like dumb, driven cattle!
　Be a hero in the strife!

Trust no Future howe'er pleasant,
　Let the dead Past bury its dead!
Act,—act in the living Present!
　Heart within, and God o'erhead!

Lives of great men all remind us
　We can make our lives sublime,
And, departing, leave behind us
　Footprints on the sands of Time;—

Footprints, that perhaps another,
　Sailing o'er life's solemn main,
A forlorn and shipwrecked brother,
　Seeing, shall take heart again.

Let us, then, be up and doing,
　With a heart for any fate;
Still achieving, still pursuing,
　Learn to labor and to wait.
　　　　　　Henry W. Longfellow.

THE FAIRY WEDDING.

Last night I heard the bluebells ring,
　For a fairy wedding,
And then the sound of fairy feet,
　Through my garden treading.

A soft and merry pattering.
  As if rain were falling:
And then their voices small and shrill.
  To one another calling.

And little laughter, like the trill
  Of a baby linnet
That tries the song his mother sings,
  And cannot well begin it.

I pushed aside the trumpet vine
  To my casement clinging.
And thus dislodged a fairy man,
  In a blossom swinging.

And then I saw the bridal train
  Down the pathway going:
Six little fairies went before.
  Fresh flowers about them throwing.

The bridegroom wore a trailing robe
  Made of red carnations,
And, as he walked, the air was full
  Of fairy acclamations:

And fairy lanterns brightly glowed
  From the bushes hanging:
And honeysuckle trumpets made
  A loud and joyful clanging.

The bride beside the bridegroom walked
  Beautiful and tender:
Her dress, a lily cup, was trimmed
  In height of fairy splendor.

With bluebirds' down her wrists were
    bound.
  Caught at early morning:
The yellow-girdled wasp had given
  His belt for her adorning.

Her kerchief was of spider lace,
    Her shoes were mouse's leather;
And, nodding on her head, she wore
    A golden robin's feather.

The merry bluebells rang again,
    Ne'er was such a pealing;
And all the fairy lanterns glowed,
    The fairy train revealing.

And at the crimson rose's foot
    Fays in crowds assembled,
And with the weight of fairy men,
    Its leaves and blossoms trembled.

Some sat within the lily cups,
    Some swung on the grasses;
And some cool dewdrops carried round,
    In tiny crystal glasses.

As o'er the window ledge I leaned,
    At the fairies gazing,
I quite forgot my face to hide
    The sight was so amazing.

And suddenly a sharp-eyed fay
    Saw me—there was a bustle,
And then the garden walks were still
    Save for the night wind's rustle.

The firefly lamps no longer glowed,
    I heard no fairies treading;—
And so I cannot tell you all
    About a fairy wedding.
               Amelia Daley Alden.

HIGH-TIDE ON THE COAST OF LINCOLNSHIRE.

The old mayor climbed the belfry tower,
    The ringers ran by two, by three;
"Pull! if ye never pulled before;
    Good ringers, pull your best," quoth he.

"Play uppe, play uppe, O Boston bells!
Ply all your changes, all your swells!
Play uppe *The Brides of Enderby!*"

Men say it was a "stolen tyde,"—
The Lord that sent it, He knows all,
But in myne ears doth still abide
The message that the bells let fall;
And there was naught of strange, beside
The flights of mews and peevits pied,
By millions crouched on the old sea-wall.

I sat and spun within the doore;
My thread brake off, I raised myne eyes;
The level sun, like ruddy ore,
Lay sinking in the barren skies;
And dark against day's golden death
She moved where Lindis wandereth,—
My sonne's faire wife, Elizabeth.

"Cusha! Cusha! Cusha!" calling,
Ere the early dews were falling,
Farre away I heard her song.
"Cusha! Cusha!" all along;
Where the reedy Lindis floweth,
Floweth, floweth,
From the meads where melick groweth,
Faintly came her milking-song:

"Cusha! Cusha! Cusha!" calling,
"For the dews will soon be falling,
Leave your meadow grasses mellow,
Mellow, mellow!
Quit your cowslips, cowslips yellow!
Come uppe, Whitefoot! come uppe,
Lightfoot!
Quit the stalks of parsley hollow,
Hollow, hollow!
Come uppe, Jetty! rise and follow;
From the clovers lift your head!
Come uppe, Whitefoot! come uppe,
Lightfoot!

Come uppe, Jetty! rise and follow,
Jetty, to the milking-shed."

If it be long—ay, long ago—
  When I beginne to think howe long,
Againe I hear the Lindis flow,
  Swift as an arrowe, sharpe and strong;
And all the aire, it seemeth mee,
Bin full of floating bells (sayth shee),
That ring the tune of *Enderby.*

Alle fresh the level pasture lay,
  And not a shadow mote be seene,
Save where, full fyve good miles away,
  The steeple towered from out the greene.
And lo! the great bell faree and wide
Was heard in all the country-side
That Saturday at eventide.

The swanherds where their sedges are,
  Moved on in sunset's golden breath;
The shepherde lads I heard afarre,
  And my sonne's wife Elizabeth;
Till, floating o'er the grassy sea,
Came downe that kyndly message free,
The Brides of Mavis Enderby.

Then some looked uppe into the sky,
  And all along where Lindis flows
To where the goodly vessels lie,
  And where the lordly steeple shows.
They sayde, "And why should this thing be?
What danger lowers by land or sea?
They ring the tune of *Enderby.*

"For evil news from Mabelthorpe,
  Of pyrate galleys, warping down,—
For ships ashore beyond the scorpe,
  They have not spared to wake the towne;
But while the west bin red to see,
And storms be none, and pyrates flee,
Why ring *The Brides of Enderby?*"

I looked without, and lo! my sonne
  Came riding downe with might and main;
He raised a shout as he drew on,
  Till all the welkin rang again:
"Elizabeth! Elizabeth!"
(A sweeter woman ne'er drew breath
Than my sonne's wife, Elizabeth.)

"The olde sea-wall," he cryed, "is downe!
  The rising tide comes on apace;
And boats adrift in yonder towne
  Go sailing uppe the market-place!"
He shook as one that looks on death;
"God save you, mother!" straight he sayth;
"Where is my wife, Elizabeth?"

"Good sonne, where Lindis winds away
  With her two bairns I marked her long;
And ere yon bells beganne to play,
  Afar I heard her milking-song."
He looked across the grassy sea,
To right, to left, Ho, Enderby!
They rang The Brides of Enderby.

With that he cried and beat his breast;
  For lo! along the river's bed
A mighty eygre reared his crest,
  And uppe the Lindis raging sped.
It swept with thunderous noises loud,—
Shaped like a curling snow-white cloud,
Or like a demon in a shroud.

And rearing Lindis, backward pressed,
  Shook all her trembling bankes amaine;
Then madly at the eygre's breast
  Flung uppe her weltering walls again.
Then bankes came downe with ruin and rout,—
Then beaten foam flew round about,—
Then all the mighty floods were out.

So farre, so fast, the eygre drave,
   The heart had hardly time to beat
Before a shallow seething wave
   Sobbed in the grasses at oure feet;
The feet had hardly time to flee
Before it brake against the knee,—
And all the world was in the sea.

Upon the roofe we sate that night;
   The noise of bells went sweeping by;
I marked the lofty beacon light
   Stream from the church tower, red and
     high,—
A lurid mark, and dread to see;
And awsome bells they were to mee,
That in the dark rang *Enderby*.

They rang the sailor lads to guide,
   From roofe to roofe who fearless rowed;
And I,—my sonne was at my side,
   And yet the ruddy beacon glowed;
And yet he moaned beneath his breath,
"O, come in life, or come in death!
O lost! my love, Elizabeth!"

And didst thou visit him no more?
   Thou didst, thou didst, my daughter deare;
The waters laid thee at his doore
   Ere yet the early dawn was cleare:
Thy pretty bairns in fast embrace,
The lifted sun shone on thy face,
Downe drifted to thy dwelling-place.

That *flowe* strewed wrecks about the grass,
   That *ebbe* swept out the flocks to sea,—
A fatal *ebbe* and *flowe*, alas!
   To manye more than myne and mee;
But each will mourn his own (she sayth)
And sweeter woman ne'er drew breath
Than my sonne's wife, Elizabeth.

I shall never hear her more
By the reedy Lindis shore,
"Cusha! Cusha! Cusha!" calling,
Ere the early dews be falling;
I shall never hear her song,
"Cusha! Cusha!" all along,
Where the sunny Lindis floweth,
  Goeth, floweth,
From the meads where melick groweth,
Where the water, winding down,
Onward floweth to the town.

I shall never see her more,
Where the reeds and rushes quiver,
  Shiver, quiver,
Stand beside the sobbing river,—
Sobbing, throbbing, in its falling
To the sandy, lonesome shore;
I shall never hear her calling,
"Leave your meadow grasses mellow,
  Mellow, mellow!
Quit your cowslips, cowslips yellow!
Come uppe, Whitefoot, come uppe, Lightfoot!
Quit your pipes of parsley hollow,
  Hollow, hollow!
Come uppe, Lightfoot! rise and follow,
  Lightfoot! Whitefoot!
From your clovers lift the head;
Come uppe, Jetty! follow, follow,
  Jetty, to the milking-shed!"
            Jean Ingelow.

BUTTERCUPS AND DAISIES.

BUTTERCUPS and daisies, oh, the pretty flowers!
Coming ere the spring-time to tell of sunny hours.

While the trees are leafless, while the fields
    are bare,
Buttercups and daisies spring up here and
    there.

Ere the snow-drop peepeth, ere the crocus
    bold,
Ere the early primrose opes its paly gold;
Somewhere on a sunny bank buttercups are
    bright!
Somewhere 'mong the frozen grass peeps the
    daisy white.

Little hardy flowers, like to children poor
Playing in their sturdy health by their
    mother's door;
Purple with the north-wind, yet alert and
    bold,
Fearing not and caring not, though they be
    a-cold!

What to them is weather, what are stormy
    showers!
Buttercups and daisies are these human
    flowers!
He who gave them hardship and a life of
    care,
Gave them likewise hardy strength and
    patient hearts to bear.

Welcome, yellow buttercups! welcome, daisies
    white!
Ye are in my spirit visioned, a delight!
Coming ere the spring-time, of sunny hours
    to tell—
Speaking to our hearts of Him who doeth all
    things well.

Mary Hewitt.

SONG OF THE BROOK.

I COME from haunts of coot and hern:
  I make a sudden sally
And sparkle out among the fern,
  To bicker down a valley.

By thirty hills I hurry down,
  Or slip between the ridges,
By twenty thorps, a little town,
  And half a hundred bridges.

Till last by Philip's farm I flow
  To join the brimming river,
For men may come and men may go,
  But I go on forever.

I chatter over stony ways,
  In little sharps and trebles.
I bubble into eddying bays,
  I babble on the pebbles.

With many a curve my banks I fret
  By many a field and fallow,
And many a fairy foreland set
  With willow-weed and mallow.

I chatter, chatter as I flow
  To join the brimming river:
For men may come and men may go,
  But I go on forever.

I wind about, and in and out,
  With here a blossom sailing,
And here and there a lusty trout,
  And here and there a grayling.

And here and there a foamy flake
  Upon me, as I travel
With many a silver waterbreak
  Above the golden gravel,

And draw them all along, and flow
To join the brimming river,
For men may come and men may go,
But I go on forever.

I steal by lawns and grassy plots:
I slide by hazel covers;
I move the sweet forget-me-nots
That grow for happy lovers.

I slip, I slide, I gloom, I glance.
Among my skimming swallows.
I make the nettled sunbeams dance
Against my sandy shallows.

I murmur under moon and stars
In brambly wildernesses;
I linger by my shingly bars;
I loiter round my cresses;

And out again I curve and flow
To join the brimming river,
For men may come and men may go,
But I go on forever.
Alfred Tennyson.

WILD GEESE.

The wind blows, the sun shines, the birds sing loud,
The blue, blue sky is flecked with fleecy dappled cloud,
Over earth's rejoicing fields the children dance and sing,
And the frogs pipe in chorus, "It is spring! it is spring!"

The grass comes, the flower laughs where lately lay the snow,
O'er the breezy hill-top hoarsely calls the crow,

By the flowing river the alder catkins swing,
And the sweet song-sparrow cries, "Spring!
  it is spring!"

Hark, what a clamor goes winging through
  the sky!
Look, children! Listen to the sound so wild
  and high!
Like a peal of broken bells,—kling, klang,
  kling,—
Far and high the wild geese cry, "Spring! it
  is spring!"

Bear the winter off with you, O wild geese
  dear!
Carry all the cold away, far away from here;
Chase the snow into the north, O strong of
  heart and wing,
While we share the robin's rapture, crying,
  "Spring! it is spring!"
  Celia Thaxter, in "St. Nicholas."

THE TRADESPEOPLE.

THE swallow is a mason;
  And underneath the eaves
He builds a nest, and plasters it
  With mud and hay and leaves.

The woodpecker is hard at work:
  A carpenter is he:
And you may find him hammering
  His house high up a tree.

The bullfinch knows and practices
  The basketmaker's trade:
See what a cradle for his young
  The little thing has made!

Of all the weavers that I know,
  The chaffinch is the best;
High on the apple-tree he weaves
  A cosy little nest.

The goldfinch is a fuller:
  A skilful workman he!
Of wool and threads he makes a nest
  That you would like to see.

The cuckoo laughs to see them work:
  "Not so," he says, "we do:
My wife and I take others' nests,
  And live at ease—cuckoo!"
Julius Sturm.

TAKE CARE.

LITTLE children, you must seek
  Rather to be good than wise,
For the thoughts you do not speak
  Shine out in your cheeks and eyes.

If you think that you can be
  Cross or cruel, and look fair,
Let me tell you how to see
  You are quite mistaken there.

Go and stand before the glass,
  And some ugly thought contrive,
And my word will come to pass
  Just as sure as you're alive!

What you have and what you lack,
  All the same as what you wear,
You will see reflected back,
  So, my little folks, take care!

And not only in the glass
  Will your secrets come to view,
All beholders, as they pass,
  Will perceive and know them too.

Out of sight, my boys and girls,
  Every root of beauty starts;
So think less about your curls,
  More about your minds and hearts.

Cherish what is good, and drive
  Evil thoughts and feelings far;
For, as sure as you're alive,
  You will show for what you are.
            Alice Cary.

SIR PATRICK SPENS.

THE king in Dunfermline town,
  Drinking the blude-red wine;
"O whare will I get a sailor gude,
  To sail this ship of mine?"

O up and spake an eldern knight,
  Sat at the king's right knee—
"Sir Patrick Spens is the best sailor
  That ever sailed the sea."

Our king has written a braid letter,
  And sealed it with his hand,
And sent it to Sir Patrick Spens,
  Was walking on the strand.

"To Noroway, to Noroway,
  To Noroway o'er the faem,
The king's daughter of Noroway,
  'Tis thou man bring her hame."

The first word that Sir Patrick read,
  Sae loud, loud laughed he,
The neist word that Sir Patrick read,
  The tear blinded his e'e.

"O wha is this has done this deed,
  And tauld the king o' me,
To send us out, at this time o' year—
  To sail upon the sea?

"Be it wind, be it weet, be it hail, be it sleet,
  Our ship must sail the faem
The king's daughter of Noroway,
  'Tis we must fetch her hame."

They hoysed their sails on Mononday morn,
  Wi' a' the speed they may;
They hae landed in Noroway;
  Upon a Wodensday,

* * * * * * *

"Make ready, make ready, my merry men a'!
  Our gude ship sails the morn,"
"Now ever alake, my master dear;
  I fear a deadly storm!

"I saw the new moon late yestreen,
  Wi' the auld moon in her arm;
And, if we gang to sea, master,
  I fear we'll come to harm."

They had nae sailed a league, a league,
  A league but barely three,
When the lift grew dark and the wind blew loud,
  And gurly grew the sea.

The ankers brak, and the topmasts lap,
    It was sic a deadly storm;
And the waves cam o'er the broken ship,
    Till a' her sides were torn.

" O where will I get a gude sailor,
    To take my helm in hand,
Till I get up to the tall topmast;
    To see if I can spy land ? "

" O here am I, a sailor gude,
    To take this helm in hand,
Till you go up to the tall topmast,
    But I fear you'll ne'er spy land."

He hadna gane a step, a step,
    A step but barely ane,
When a bout flew out of our goodly ship,
    And the salt sea it came in.

" Gae fetch a web o' the silken claith,
    Another o' the twine:
And wap them into our ship's side,
    But let nae the sea come in."

They fetched a web o' the silken claith,
    Another o' the twine
And they wrapped them round that
    good ship's side,
But still the leak came in.

O laith, laith, were our gude Scots lords
    To weet their shining shoon!
But lang ar a' the play was played
    They wat their hats aboon.

And mony was the feather bed,
    That fluttered o'er the faem:
And mony was the good lord's son,
    That never mare cam hame.

The ladyes wrang their fingers white,
  The maidens tore their hair,
A' for the sake of their true loves,
  For them they'll see nae mair.

O lang, lang, may the ladyes sigh,
  Wi' their fans int their hand,
Before they see Sir Patrick Spens
  Come sailing to the strand!

And lang, lang may the maidens sit,
  With their gold kaims in their hair,
A' waiting for their ain dear loves!
  For them they'll nae see mair.

It's half way over to Aberdour,
  'Tis fifty fathoms deep,
And there Sir Patrick lies for aye,
  Wi' the Scots lords at his feet.
                      An Old Ballad.

THE DESTRUCTION OF SENNACHERIB.

THE Assyrian came down like the wolf on the fold,
And the cohorts were gleaming in purple and gold;
And the sheen of their spears was like stars on the sea,
When the blue waves roll nightly on deep Galilee.

Like the leaves of the forest when summer is green,
That host with their banners at sunset were seen;

Like the leaves of the forest when autumn
   hath blown,
That host on the morrow lay withered and
   strown.

For the Angel of Death spread his wings on
   the blast,
And breathed in the face of the foe as he
   passed;
And the eyes of the sleepers waxed deadly
   and chill,
And their hearts but once heaved, and forever
   grew still!

And there lay the steed with his nostrils all
   wide,
But through it there rolled not the breath of
   his pride:
And the foam of his gasping lay white on the
   turf,
And cold as the spray of the rock-beating
   surf.

And there lay the rider, distorted and pale,
With the dew on his brow and the rust on
   his mail;
And the tents were all silent, the banners
   alone,
The lances unlifted, the trumpets unblown.

And the widows of Ashur are loud in their
   wail,
And the idols are broke in the temple of Baal;
And the might of the Gentile, unsmote by the
   sword,
Hath melted like snow in the glance of the
   Lord!

Byron.

THE BETTER LAND.

"I HEAR thee speak of the better land,
Thou call'st its children a happy band;
Mother! O where is that radiant shore?
Shall we not seek it and weep no more?
Is it where the flower of the orange blows,
And the fire-flies glance thro' the myrtle
    boughs?"
—"Not there, not there, my child!"

"Is it where the feathery palm-trees rise,
And the date grows ripe under sunny skies?
Or midst the green islands of glittering seas,
Where fragrant forests perfume the breeze,
And strange, bright birds, on starry wings,
Bear the rich hues of all glorious things?"
—"Not there, not there, my child!"

"Is it far away in some region old,
Where the rivers wander o'er sands of gold?
Where the burning rays of the ruby shine,
And the diamond lights up the secret mine,
And the pearl gleams forth from the coral
    strand?
Is it there, sweet mother! that better land?"
—"Not there, not there, my child!"

"Eye hath not seen it, my gentle boy!
Ear hath not heard its deep songs of joy;
Dreams cannot picture a world so fair—
Sorrow and death may not enter there;
Time doth not breathe on its fadeless bloom,
For beyond the clouds, and beyond the tomb,
—It is there, it is there, my child!"
            Felicia Hemans.

THE KING SPEAKS.
A BOY'S FANCY.

My gold is in the sunlight, and my silver in
the moon,
And my jewels are the dew-drops that deck
the green of June;
My castle is a shady nook within the forest
glade;
My throne a mound of blue and green of
blooming myrtle made;
I wear a crown of daisies, and my scepter is a
reed;
My robe is trimmed with lichens and with
downy thistle-seed;
And wide as is the woodland is the breadth of
my domain,—
My viaducts the forest paths, my aqueducts,
the rain;
My bridges are the fallen trees that o'er the
brooklets lie;
My monuments the beetling crags that frown
against the sky.

The cities in my kingdom are all peopled by
the birds,
By squirrels, and by katy-dids, and soft-eyed,
browsing herds;
My courtiers are the dragon-flies that in the
sunlight gleam;
My navies are the fallen leaves that float
adown the stream;
My color-bearers, butter-flies; the ants, my
armied men;
The robin is my herald, and my messenger,
the wren.

When I give an entertainment, my banquet-
board is spread

With berries of the wintergreen, and nuts, and
  apples red,
And dainty cups of acorns, and plates of
  plantain leaves;
My curtains are the gauzy webs the giant
  spider weaves.
My mirror is the shady pool where water-
  lilies lie;
My pictures are the hills and vales, the blue
  or stormy sky;
My orchestra the wildwood birds that sing at
  set of sun;
My chandeliers the fire-flies that glow when
  day is done;
To guard my quiet sleep, the night her starry
  sentries gives;
In sweet content I know I am the richest king
  that lives.
                    WILL H. VEITH, in *Good Cheer*.

CASABIANCA.

THE boy stood on the burning deck,
  Whence all but him had fled;
The flame that lit the battle's wreck
  Shone round him o'er the dead.

Yet beautiful and bright he stood,
  As born to rule the storm;
A creature of heroic blood,
  A proud though child-like form.

The flames rolled on; he would not go
  Without his father's word;
That father, faint in death below,
  His voice no longer heard.

He called aloud, "Say, father, say,
  If yet my task be done?"
He knew not that the chieftan lay
  Unconscious of his son.

His charge is the whirlwind that scatters the
   foe.

How grandly and nobly he stands to his
   trust,
When, roused at the call of a course that is
   just,
He weds his strong will to the valor of youth,
And writes on his banner the watchword of
   Truth!

Then up and be doing! the day is not long;
Throw fear to the winds, be patient and
   strong!
Stand fast in your place, act your part like a
   man,
And, when duty calls, answer promptly, "*I
   Can.*"
   WILLIAM ALLEN BUTLER.

BABY BYE.

BABY Bye,
Here's a fly;
Let us watch him you and I.
   How he crawls
   Up the walls,
   Yet he never falls!
I believe with six such legs
You and I could walk on eggs.
   There he goes
   On his toes
   Tickling Baby's nose.

Spots of red
Dot his head;
Rainbows on his back are spread:
   That small speck,
   Is his neck;
   See him nod and beck.
I can show you if you choose,

Where to look to find his shoes;—
   Three small pairs,
   Made of hairs;
   These he always wears.

 Black and brown
 Is his gown;
 He can wear it upside-down;
   It is laced
   Round his waist;
   I admire his taste.
Yet though tight his clothes are made,
He will lose them, I'm afraid,
   If to-night
   He gets sight
   Of the candle-light.

 In the sun
 Webs are spun;
 What if he gets into one?
   When it rains
   He complains
   On the window-panes.
Tongue to talk have you and I;
God has given the little fly
   No such things,
   So he sings
   With his buzzing wings.

 He can eat
 Bread and meat;
 There's his mouth between his feet.
   On his back
   Is a pack
   Like a peddler's sack.
Does the baby understand?
Then the fly shall kiss her hand;
   Put a crumb
   On her thumb,
   Maybe he will come.

"Speak, father!" once again he cried,
  "If I may yet be gone!"
And but the booming shots replied,
  And fast the flames rolled on.

Upon his brow he felt their breath,
  And in his waving hair,
And looked from that lone post of death
  In still yet brave despair;

And shouted but once more aloud,
  "My father! must I stay?"
While o'er him fast, through sail and
    shroud,
  The wreathing fires made way.

They wrapt the ship in splendor wild,
  They caught the flag on high,
And streamed above the gallant child,
  Like banners in the sky.

There came a burst of thunder sound;
  The boy,——Oh, where was *he?*
Ask of the winds, that far around
  With fragments strewed the sea,—

With shroud and mast and pennon fair,
  That well had borne their part,—
But the noblest thing that perished there
  Was that young, faithful heart.

FELICIA HEMANS.

GIANT AND DWARF.

As on through life's journey we go day by day,
There are two whom we meet, at each turn of the way,
To help or to hinder, to bless or to ban,—
And the names of the two are "*I Can't*" and "*I Can.*"

"*I Can't*" is a dwarf, a poor, pale, puny imp,
His eyes are half blind, and his walk is a limp;
He stumbles and falls, or lies writhing with fear,
Though dangers are distant and succor is near.

"*I Can*" is a giant; unbending he stands;
There is strength in his arms and skill in his hands;
He asks for no favors; he wants but a share
Where labor is honest and wages are fair.

"*I Can't*" is a sluggard, too lazy to work·
From duty he shrinks, every task he will shirk;
No bread on his board and no meal in his bag;
His house is a ruin, his coat is a rag.

"*I Can*" is a worker; he tills the broad fields,
And digs from the earth all the wealth which it yields;
The hum of his spindles begins with the light,
And the fires of his forges are blazing all night.

"*I Can't*" is a coward, half fainting with fright;
At the first thought of peril he slinks out of sight;
Skulks and hides till the noise of the battle is past,
Or sells his best friend, and turns traitor at last.

"*I Can*" is a hero, the first in the field;
Though others may falter, he never will yield;
He makes the long marches, he deals the last blow,

Catch him? No,
Let him go,
Never hurt an insect so;
    But no doubt
    He flies out
    Just to gad about.
Now you see his wings of silk
Drabbled in the baby's milk;
    Fie, O fie,
    Foolish fly!
    How will he get dry?

All wet flies
Twist their thighs;
Thus they wipe their heads and eyes;
    Cats, you know,
    Wash just so,
    Then their whiskers grow.
Flies have hair too short to comb,
So they fly bareheaded home;
    But the gnat
    Wears a hat,
    Do you believe that?

Flies can see
More than we.
So how bright their eyes must be!
    Little fly
    Ope your eye;
    Spiders are near by.
For a secret I can tell, —
Spiders never use flies well.
    Then away
    Do not stay.
    Little fly, good-day.
            THEODORE TILTON.

KATY.

KATY on the doorstep sat,
While her dimpled fingers fat
Moved industrious to and fro
O're the gay pink calico;
For an apron she was making,
All herself, with much painstaking.

Pretty picture made she there,
Humming a quaint Celtic air,
Blue eyes on the work intent,
Cheek where tan and roses blent,
Brown hair smoothly brushed and
   braided,
Tied at ends with ribbon faded.

Such a happy little maid,
Sitting in the porch's shade,
Tempted me to questioning,
Till she fell a-gossiping,
All about her country telling
And the peasant's mode of dwelling;

How she came from "ferninst Corrk
Tin miles," how she used to walk
There and back without a rest,
Only, by the way confessed,
That the miles "beyant" "air shorrter"
Than they are this side the water;

How the houses are of clay,
And the roofs are green alway—
Thatched with turf; how very sweet
The odor of the burning peat,
Which warms in winter-time the cottage
And cooks the oatmeal or the pottage;

How now and then a troop passed by,
Fox-hunting, riding gallantly—
Fair ladies and fine gentlemen,
Who dashed through field, and wood,
  and glen—
Nor hedge, nor fence, nor stream could
  stay
Their fiery steeds upon the way;

How on a hill-side near her home
There stands a ruin, ivy-grown,
Which long, and long, and long gone by
Was a grand castle, strong and high;
And now by night the people passing
Make haste, for fear a ghost be chasing.

Thus and so did Katy chat,
As in the shaded porch she sat.
The little maiden twelve years old
With ready tongue her story told,
Better than all the books relate it
Or half the travelers can state it.
ELLEN TRACY ALDEN.

THE MOTHERLESS TURKEYS.

THE White Turkey was dead ! The White
  Turkey was dead!
How the news through the barn-yard went
  flying!
Of a mother bereft, four small turkeys were
  left,
And their case for assistance was crying.
E'en the Peacock respectfully folded his tail,
As a suitable symbol of sorrow,
And his plainer wife said, "Now the old bird
  is dead,
Who will tend her poor chicks on the mor-
  row ?
And when evening around them comes dreary
  and chill

Who above them will watchfully hover?"
"Two, each night, *I* will tuck 'neath my
　wings," said the Duck,
Though I've eight of my own I must cover!"
"I have *so much* to do! For the bugs and the
　worms,
In the garden, 't is tiresome pickin';
I have nothing to spare,—for my own I must
　care,"
Said the Hen with one chicken.

"How I wish," said the Goose, "I could be of
　some use,
For my heart is with love over-brimming;
The next morning that's fine they shall go
　　with my nine
Little yellow-backed goslings. out swim-
　　ming!"

"I will do what I can," the old Dorking put
　in,
"And for help they may call upon me too,
Though I've ten of my own that are only half
　grown,
And a great deal of trouble to see to.
But those poor little things, they are all heads
　and wings,
And their bones through their feathers are
　stickin'!"
"Very hard it may be, but, O don't come to
　me!"
Said the Hen with one chicken.

"Half my care, I suppose, there is nobody
　knows,—
I'm the most overburdened of mothers!
They must learn, little elves! how to scratch
　for themselves,
And not seek to depend upon others."
She went by with a cluck, and the Goose to
　the Duck

Exclaimed, in surprise, "Well, I never!"
Said the Duck, "I declare, those who have
    the best care,
You will find are complaining forever!
And when all things appear to be threatening
    and drear,
And when troubles your pathway are thick
    in,
For some aid in your woe, O, beware how
    you go
To a Hen with one chicken!"

MARIAN DOUGLASS.

TINY TOKENS.

THE murmur of a waterfall
  A mile away,
The rustle when a robin lights
  Upon a spray,
The lapping of a lowland stream
  On dipping boughs,
The sound of grazing from a herd
  Of gentle cows,
The echo from a wooded hill
  Of cuckoo's call,
The quiver through the meadow grass
  At evening fall:—
Too subtle are these harmonies
  For pen and rule;
Such music is not understood
  By any school;
But when the brain is overwrought
  It hath a spell,
Beyond all human skill and power
  To make it well.

The memory of a kindly word
  Far long gone by,
The fragrance of a fading flower
  Sent lovingly,

The gleaming of a sudden smile
  Or sudden tear,
The warmer pressure of a hand,
  The tone of cheer,
The hush that means, "I cannot speak,
  But I have heard!"
The note that only bears a verse
  From God's own Word:—
Such tiny things we hardly count
  As ministry;
The givers deeming they have shown
  Scant sympathy;
But when the heart is overwrought,
  Oh, who can tell
The power of such tiny things
  To make it well?
FRANCES RIDLEY HAVERGAL.

THE SONG OF STEAM.

HARNESS me down with your iron bands,
  Be sure of your curb and rein,
For I scorn the strength of your puny hands
  As a tempest scorns a chain.
How I laughed as I lay concealed from sight
  For many a countless hour,
At the childish boasts of human might,
  And the pride of human power.

When I saw an army upon the land,
  A navy upon the seas
Creeping along, a snail-like band,
  Or waiting a wayward breeze:
When I saw the weary peasant reel
  With the toil that he faintly bore,
As he turned all day at the tardy wheel,
  Or toiled at the weary oar:

When I measured the panting courser's speed
  The flight of the carrier dove,

As they bore a law the King decreed,
   Or the lines of impatient love,
I could but think how the world would feel
   As these were outstripped afar,
When I should be bound to the rushing keel,
   Or chained to the flying car!

Ha! ha! ha! They found me at last,
   They invited me forth at length,
And I rushed to my throne with a thunder
     blast,
   And laughed in my iron strength!
Oh! there ye saw a wonderous change
   On the earth and ocean wide,
Where now my fiery armies range,
   Nor wait for wind nor tide.

Hurrah! hurrah! the waters o're
   The mountain steep decline;
Time—space—have yielded to my power-
   The world! the world is mine!
The rivers the sun hath earliest blest,
   Or those where his beams decline;
The giant streams of the queenly West,
   Or the Orient floods divine.

The ocean gales where'er I sweep
   To hear my strength rejoice,
And monsters of the briny deep
   Cower trembling at my voice.
I carry the wealth and worth of earth,
   The thought of the God like mind:
The wind lags after my going forth,
   The lightning is left behind.

In the darksome depths of the fathomless
     mine,
   My tireless arm doth play.
Where the rocks ne'er saw the sun's decline
   Or the dawn of the glorious day;
I bring earth's glittering jewels up
   From the hidden caves below.

And I make the fountain's granite cup
    With a crystal gush o'erflow.
I blow the bellows, I forge the steel
    In all the shops of trade;
I hammer the ore and turn the wheel
    Where my arms of strength are made;
I manage the furnace, the mill, the mint—
    I carry, I spin, I weave,
And all my doings I put in print
    On every Saturday eve.

I've no muscles to weary, no breath to decay,
    No bones to be "laid on the shelf,"
And soon I intend you may "go and play,"
    While I manage the world myself.
But harness me down with your iron bands,
    Be sure of your curb and rein,
For I scorn the strength of your puny hands
    As the tempest scorns the chain.
                                G. W. CUTTER.

THE LAST HYMN.

THE Sabbath day was ending at a village by
    the sea,
The uttered benediction touched the people
    tenderly;
And they rose to face the sunlight in the
    glowing, lighted West,
And then hastened to their dwellings for
    God's blessed boon of rest.

But they looked across the waters and a
    storm was raging there:
A fierce spirit moved above them—the wild
    spirit of the air;
And it lashed and shook and tore them, till
    they thundered, groaned and boomed:
And alas! for any vessel in their yawning
    gulfs entombed.

Very anxious were the people on that rocky
coast of Wales,
Lest the dawns of coming morrows should be
telling awful tales.
When the sea had spent its passion, and
cast upon the shore
Bits of wreck and swollen victims, as it oft
had done before.

With the rough winds blowing round her, a
brave woman strained her eyes,
And she saw along the billows the large vessel fall and rise.
Oh! it did not need a prophet to tell what the
end must be,
For no ship could ride in safety near the
shore, on such a sea.

Then the pitying people hurried from their
homes and thronged the beach:
Oh! for power to cross the waters and the
perishing to reach!
Helpless hands were wrung for sorrow, tender hearts grew cold with dread;
And the ship, urged by the tempest, to the
fatal rock-shore sped.

She has parted in the middle! Oh! the half of
her goes down!
God have mercy! "Say, is Heaven far to seek
for those who drown?"
Lo! when next the white shocked faces looked
with terror on the sea,
Only one last clinging figure on the spar was
seen to be.

Nearer the trembling watchers came the
wreck, tossed by the wave,
And the man still clung and floated, though
no power on earth could save.
"Could we send him a short message? Here's
a trumpet—shout away!"

'Twas the preacher's hand that took it, and
he wondered what to say.

Any memory of his sermon? Firstly? Secondly? Ah no!
There was but one thing to utter, in the awful hour of woe;
So he shouted through the trumpet, "Look to Jesus! Can you hear?"
And "Ay, ay, sir," rang the answer o'er the waters loud and clear.

Then they listened: "He is singing 'Jesus, lover of my soul!'"
And the winds brought back the echo, "While the nearer waters roll."
Strange indeed it was to hear him—"Till the storm of life be past—"
Singing bravely from the waters, "Oh, receive my soul at last."

He could have no other refuge—"Hangs my helpless soul on Thee;"
"Leave, oh leave me not—" the singer dropped at last into the sea:
And the watchers looking homeward, though their eyes with tears made dim,
Said, "He passed to be with Jesus, in the singing of that hymn."

MARIANNE FARMINGHAM.

DUTIFUL JEM.

THERE was a poor widow who lived in a cot,
She scarcely a blanket to warm her had got;
Her windows were broken, her walls were all bare,
And the cold winter-wind often whistled in there.

Poor Susan was old, and too feeble to spin,
Her forehead was wrinkled, her hands they were thin:
And bread she'd have wanted as many have done,
If she had not been blessed with a good little son.

But he loved her well, like a dutiful lad,
And thought her the very best friend that he had;
And now to neglect or forsake her, he knew
Was the most wicked thing he could possibly do.

For he was quite healthy, and active, and stout,
While his poor mother hardly could waddle about,
And he thought it his duty and greatest delight,
To work for her living from morning till night.

So he started each morning as gay as a lark,
And worked all day long in the field till 'twas dark;
Then came home again to his dear mother's cot
And cheerfully gave her the wages he got.

And oh, how she loved him! how great was her joy!
To think her dear Jem was a dutiful boy;
Her arm round his neck she would tenderly cast,
And kiss his red cheek, while her tears trickled fast.

Oh, then was not little Jem happier far,
Than naughty, and idle, and wicked boys are?
For as long as he lived, 'twas his comfort
    and joy,
To think he'd not been an undutiful boy.

JANE TAYLOR.

THE BROWN THRUSH.

THERE's a merry brown thrush sitting up in
    the tree.
" He's singing to me! He's singing to me!"
And what does he say, little girl, little boy?
"O, the world's running over with joy!
Don't you hear? Don't you see? Hush! Look!
    In my tree
I'm as happy as happy can be!"

And the brown thrush keeps singing, "A
    nest do you see,
And five eggs, hid by me in the juniper-tree?
Don't meddle! don't touch! little girl, little
    boy,
Or the world will lose some of its joy!
Now I'm glad! now I'm free!
And I always shall be,
If you never bring sorrow to me."

So the merry brown thrush sings away in the
    tree,
To you and to me, to you and to me:
And he sings all the day, little girl, little boy,
" O, the world's running over with joy!
But long it won't be,
Don't you know? don't you see?
Unless we are as good as can be?"

LUCY LARCOM.

SEVEN TIMES ONE.

THERE'S no dew left on the daisies and clover,
  There's no rain left in heaven.
I've said my "seven times" over and over,—
  Seven times one are seven.

I am old,—so old I can write a letter;
  My birthday lessons are done.
The lambs play always,—they know no better;
  They are only one times one.

O Moon! in the night I have seen you sailing
  And shining so round and low.
You were bright—ah, bright— but your light
    is failing;
  You are nothing now but a bow.

You Moon! have you done something wrong
    in heaven,
  That God has hidden your face?
I hope, if you have, you will soon be forgiven,
  And shine again in your place.

O velvet Bee! you're a dusty fellow,—
  You've powdered your legs with gold.
O brave marsh Mary buds, rich and yellow,
  Give me your money to hold!

O Columbine! open your folded wrapper,
  Where two twin turtle-doves dwell!
O Cuckoo-pint! toll me the purple clapper
  That hangs in your clear green bell!

And show me your nest, with the young ones
    in it,—
  I will not steal them away:
I am old! you may trust me, linnet, linnet!
  I am seven times one to-day.
                    JEAN INGELOW.

THE HEAVENLY FRIEND.

I HAVE a Friend! a precious Friend, unchanging, wise, and true,
The chief among ten thousand! O, I wish you knew him too!
Encompassed by a host of foes, weary in heart and limb,
I know who waits to soothe my woe: have you a Friend like him?
He comforts me, he strengthens me; how can I then repine?
He loveth me! This faithful Friend in life and death is mine.

I have a Father, true and fond! He cares for all my needs;
His patience bore my faithless ways, my mad and foolish deeds;
To me he sends sweet messages: he waiteth but to bless;
Have you a Father like to mine, with such deep tenderness?
For me a kingdom doth he keep, for me a crown is won;
I was a rebel once. He calls the rebel child his son.

I have a proved, unerring Guide! whose love I often grieve,
He brings me golden promises my heart can scarce receive;
He leadeth me, and hope and cheer doth for my path provide,
For dreary nights and days of drought; have you so sure a Guide?
Quench not the faintest whisper that the heavenly Dove may bring,
He seeks with holy love to lure the wanderer 'neath his wing.

I have a home, a home so bright, its beauties
   none can know;
Its sapphire pavements, and such palms—
   none ever saw below;
Its golden streets resound with joy, its pearly
   gates with praise;
A temple standeth in the midst no human
   hands could raise;
And there unfailing fountains flow, and
   pleasures never end.
Who makes that home so glorious? It is my
   loving Friend!

My Friend, my Father, and my Guide, and
   this our radiant home.
Are offered you. Turn not away! to-day, I
   pray you, "come."
My Father yearns to welcome you, his heart,
   his house, his share:
My Friend is yours, my home is yours; my
   Guide will lead you there;
Behold one altogether fair, the Faithful and
   the True?
He pleadeth with you for your love, he gave
   his life for you.

O, leave the worthless things you seek; they
   perish in a day.
Serve now the true and living God; from
   idols turn away;
Watch for the Lord, who comes to reign;
   enter the open door;
Give him thy heart, thy broken heart: thou'lt
   ask it back no more.
Trust him for grace, and strength, and love,
   and all thy troubles end;
O, come to Jesus! and behold in him my
   loving Friend!

                        ANNA SHIPTON.

THE SIGNS OF THE SEASON.

WHAT does it mean when the bluebird flies
  Over the hills, singing sweet and clear ?
When violets peep through the blades of
    grass ?—
These are the signs that spring is here.

What does it mean when the berries are ripe?
  When butterflies flit and honey-bees hum?
When cattle stand under the shady trees?—
These are the signs that summer has come.

What does it mean when the crickets chirp,
  And away to the south-land the wild-geese
    steer ?
When apples are falling and nuts are brown?—
These are the signs that autumn is here.

What does it mean when the days are short ?
  When leaves are gone and the brooks are
    dumb?
When the fields are white with the drifting
    snows ?
These are the signs that winter has come.

The old stars set, and the new ones rise,
  And skies that were stormy grow bright
    and clear;
And so the beautiful, wonderful signs
  Go round and round with the changing
    year.
    M. E. N. HATHAWAY, in *Our Little Ones.*

THE FIRST TANGLE.

ONCE in an eastern palace wide
   A little child sat weaving;
So patiently her task she plied
The men and women at her side
   Flocked round her, almost grieving.

"How is it, little one," they said,
   "You always work so cheerly?
You never seem to break your thread
Or snarl or tangle it, instead
   Of working smooth and clearly.

"Our weaving gets so worn and soiled,
   Our silk so frayed and broken,
For all we've fretted, wept, and toiled,
We know the lovely pattern's spoiled
   Before the King has spoken."

The little child looked in their eyes,
   So full of care and trouble;
And pity chased the sweet surprise
That filled her own, as sometimes flies
   The rainbow in a bubble.

"I only go and tell the King,"
   She said, abashed and meekly,
"You know he said in everything"—
"Why, so do we!" they cried, "we bring
   Him all our troubles weekly!"

She turned her little head aside;
   A moment let them wrangle;
"Ah, but," she softly then replied,
"I go and get the knot untied
   At the first little tangle!"

O little children—weavers all!
   Our broidery we spangle
With many a tear that need not fall,

If on our King we would but call
At the first little tangle!
ANNA F. BURNHAM, in *Congregationalist.*

A BUILDER'S LESSON.

"How shall I a habit break?"
As you did that habit make.
As you gathered, you must lose;
As you yielded, now refuse.
Thread by thread the strands we twist
Till they bind us, neck and wrist;
Thread by thread the patient hand
Must untwine, ere free we stand.
As we builded, stone by stone,
We must toil, unhelped, alone,
Till the wall is overthrown.

But remember, as we try,
Lighter every test goes by;
Wading in, the stream grows deep
Toward the centre's downward sweep;
Backward turn, each step ashore
Shallower is than that before.

Ah, the precious years we waste
Levelling what we raised in haste;
Doing what must be undone
Ere content or love be won!
First, across the gulf we cast
Kite-borne threads, till lines are passed,
And habit builds the bridge at last!
JOHN BOYLE O'REILLY, in *Wide Awake.*

THE FAIRY ISLE.

A Highland Tradition.

A HIGHLAND lassie strayed alone,
  By lonely Loch Maree,
When o'er the waters came a strain
  Of fairy minstrelsie.

All things erewhile so solemn still
  Below the sailing moon,
Seemed now to wake, and throb, and thrill
  To fairy time and tune.

Beside the burnie whimpering low
  And through the darkening wood,
The lass had strayed without a fear
  To this deep solitude.

But now she holds her breath to hear
  The fairy bugles play,
While comes to her a legend heard
  In childhood's careless day.

On yon lone isle in Loch Maree,
  As ancient grandames tell,
The birk trees girdle round an isle
  Where Fairy people dwell.

And in that isle another loch
  Enfolds an isle more fair,
And underneath a wondrous tree
  The queen is throned there.

But, ah! most fearsome phantom forms
  Would mortal steps pursue,
If any heedless soul should dare
  To cross those waters blue.

Now when a gleaming fairy boat
　　Comes shimmering down the tide,
Touching the rock wheron she stood,
　　How could the lassie bide ?

How could the lassie shrink or fear?
　　How could she dream of ill?
Sure the "*good people*" are her friends—
　　She hears the music still.—

She stepped within, and o'er the flood
　　The fairy shallop sped,
And lightly touched the island beach
　　Where elfin lights gleam red;

Through all the woodland flashed the
　　　flame,
　　While onward to the shore
Of the clear inland lake she pressed,
　　And sailed its waters o'er;

And reached the isle whereon the queen
　　Beneath the wondrous tree
Sat on her throne; the lassie looked,
　　The sight was sad to see!

O'er the queen's face and o'er the throne
　　A woesome shadow fell,
The fairy music seemed to die
　　O'er heath and vale and dell.

The Highland lassie felt as one
　　Awakened from the dead,
But, pity stirred her gentle heart,
　　And to the queen she said:

"Oh, Ruler of the Fairy folk!
　　Why falls a shadow here?
Tell one who came in perfect love,
　　A love that knew no fear!"

The queen made answer, with a sigh,
  "Oh, lassie with a soul,
Condole with me, the Evil One
  Of me requireth toll.

" And from my happiest garden ground,
  And from my field most gay,
Of sweetest honey, finest fruit,
  A tithe to him I pay;

" And have no choice, who have no soul;
  But thou, oh, lassie sweet!
Mayest love the Lord on earth, in Heaven
  Mayest worship at his feet."

And deep she moaned, the Fairy Queen,
  Beneath the wondrous tree;
The lassie swooned, but waking heard
  No fairy minstrelsie.

Finding herself all, all alone,
  By lonely Loch Maree,
The fair moon sailing in the sky,
  Looked on her tenderly.

Ah! when her tale was told, who heard
  In sad and silent awe,
They never sought the isle, to see
  The sight the lassie saw.

But Highlanders this lesson kept:—
  " Who owneth not God's name,
Nor yields to him obedience,
  The Evil One may claim."

Louise V. Boyd.

THE ARAB'S FAREWELL TO HIS STEED.

My beautiful! my beautiful!
    That standest meekly by,
With thy proudly arched and glossy
    neck,
Thy dark and fiery eye—
Fret not to roam the desert now
    With all thy winged speed,
I may not mount on thee again
    Thou 'rt sold, my Arab steed!

Fret not with that impatient hoof,
    Snuff not the breezy wind;
The farther that thou fliest now,
    So far am I behind.
The stranger hath thy bridle-rein,
    Thy master hath his gold:
Fleet-winged and beautiful, farewell!
    Thou 'rt sold, my steed, thou 'rt sold!

Farewell! those free untired limbs
    Full many miles must roam,
To reach the chill and wintry sky
    Which clouds the stranger's home;
Some other hand, less fond, must now
    Thy corn and bread prepare;
Thy silken mane, I braided once,
    Must be another's care.

The morning sun shall dawn again,
    But never more with thee
Shall I go through the desert paths
    Where we were wont to be.
Evening shall darken on the earth,
    And o'er the sandy plain
Some other steed with slower step,
    Shall bear me home again.

Yes, thou must go! the wild free breeze
　　The brilliant sun and sky,
Thy master's house, from all of these
　　My exiled one must fly.
The proud, dark eye will grow less proud,
　　Thy step become less fleet,
And vainly shalt thou arch thy neck,
　　Thy master's hand to meet.

Only in sleep shall I behold
　　That dark eye glancing bright;
Only in sleep shall hear again
　　That step so firm and light;
And when I raise my dreaming arm
　　To check or cheer thy speed,
Then must I, starting, wake to feel
　　Thou 'rt sold, my Arab steed!

Ah, rudely then, unseen by me,
　　Some cruel hand may chide,
Till foam wreaths lie, like crested waves,
　　Along thy panting side;
And the rich blood that's in thee swells
　　In thy indignant pain,
Till careless eyes which rest on thee
　　May count each starting vein.

Will they ill-use thee? if I thought—
　　But no, it cannot be—
Thou art so swift yet easy curbed,
　　So gentle, yet so free.
And yet, if haply when thou 'rt gone,
　　Thy lonely heart should yearn,
Can the same hand which casts thee off
　　Command thee to return?

Return? Alas, my Arab steed,
　　What shall thy master do,
When thou who wert his all of joy
　　Hast vanished from his view?

When the dim distance cheats mine eyes,
  And through the gathering tears,
Thy bright form for a moment like
  The false mirage appears.

Slow and unmounted will I roam
  With weary foot alone.
Where with fleet step and joyous bound
  Thou oft hast borne me on;
And sitting down by that green well
  Will pause and sadly think,
'Twas here he bow'd his glossy neck,
  When last I saw him drink.

WHEN LAST I SAW HIM DRINK! Away!
  The fever'd dream is o'er,
I could not live a day, and know
  That we should meet no more.
They tempted me, my beautiful!
  For hunger's power is strong;
They tempted me, my beautiful!
  But I have loved too long.

Who said that I had given thee up?
  Who said that thou wert sold?
'Tis false, 'tis false! my Arab steed!
  I fling them back their gold.
Thus, thus I leap upon thy back,
  And scour the distant plains;
Away! Who overtakes us now
  Shall claim thee for his pains!

              Mrs. Norton.

DREAM OF THE GOLDEN AGE.

'Twas in the Golden Age;
  Turnips and trees could talk,
And roasted pigs and geese
  Could leave the plate and walk;
And apples on the trees,
  In North, or Sunny South,
Called to the lazy man:
  "I'll drop; just ope your mouth."

Folks did not rack their brains,
  For bread to eat, as now;
Or toil, with weary hands,
  And wrinkled moistened brow.
The farmer, when he wished,
  His corn and beans were planted,
Would sleep awhile, then wake
  To find his wishes granted.

The women of that day
  Ne'er browned their hands and faces,
By washing, baking bread,
  Or ironing shirts and laces.
No little chubby boys
  Were tumbled out of bed,
To chop, or feed the caloes;
  They slept till noon instead.

The girls were never called,
  To sweep, or wash the dishes;
They'd eat, then run and swing,
  Or idly watch the fishes.
No schools for boys or girls,
  No tasks, their plans o'ertipping;
No matter what they did,
  There was no fear of whipping

Brisk elfins, dressed in green,
   Or fairies robed in rose,
Were near, to soothe the child
   Who fell and bumped his nose.
And cups of bread and milk,
   And rolls of sugar candy,
If toddling urchins cried,
   Were always sitting handy.

Hats grew on stalks, like corn,
   Shoes ripened, like potatoes;
And stockings, gold and red,
   Were plenty, as tomatoes.
And all the soiled, torn clothes,
   Well patched, and washed and dried;
Hung gay, like autumn flowers,
   At morn or eventide.

No one need help his friend,
   His father, or his mother;
In time, there were no friends,
   No one who loved another.
And so the years rolled on;
   Most people, grew too lazy
Almost, to think, or eat;
   And some, grew cracked and crazy.

The children grew too dull
   And fat to run and play;
They'd sleep from morn till night,
   Or gape the time away.
At length the silver moon
   Rolled through the silent air,
So near the careless earth,
   That giants living there,
Threw nets, and caught them all;—
   Then the great moon sailed on,
With all the lazy folks,
   And the Golden Age was gone.

Persie Vere.

THE BATTLE OF BLENHEIM.

It was a summer's evening,
  Old Kaspar's work was done,
And he before his cottage door
  Was sitting in the sun;
And by him sported on the green
His little grandchild Wilhelmine.

She saw her brother Peterkin
  Roll something large and round
Which he beside the rivulet,
  In playing there, had found.
He came to ask what he had found,
That was so large, and smooth, and round.

Old Kaspar took it from the boy,
  Who stood expectant by;
And then the old man shook his head,
  And, with a natural sigh,
"'Tis some poor fellow's skull," said he,
"Who fell in the great victory.

"I find them in the garden,
  For there's many hereabout;
And often, when I go to plow,
  The plowshare turns them out;
For many thousand men," said he,
"Were slain in that great victory."

"Now tell us what 'twas all about,"
  Young Peterkin he cries;
And little Wilhelmine looks up
  With wonder-waiting eyes;
"Now tell us all about the war,
And what they killed each other for?"

"It was the English," Kaspar cried,
  "Who put the French to rout;

But what they killed each other for
   I could not well make out.
But everybody said," quoth he,
" That 'twas a famous victory !

" My father lived at Blenheim then,
   You little stream hard by;
They burned his dwelling to the ground,
   And he was forced to fly;
So with his wife and child he fled,
   Nor had he where to rest his head.

" With fire and sword the country round
   Was wasted far and wide;
And many a childing mother then
   And new born baby died.
But things like that, you know, must be
   At every famous victory.

" They say it was a shocking sight,
   After the field was won;
For many thousand bodies here
   Lay rotting in the sun.
But things like that, you know, must be
   After a famous victory.

" Great praise the Duke of Marlborough
   won,
   And our good Prince Eugene."
" Why, 'twas a very wicked thing ! "
   Said little Wilhelmine.
" Nay, nay, my little girl," quoth he,
"It was a famous victory !

" And everybody praised the duke
   Who this great fight did win."
" But what good came of it at last?
   Quoth little Peterkin.
" Why, that I cannot tell," said he,
" But 'twas a famous victory ! "

                              Robert Southey.

GRANDMA'S CORNER.

WE'LL make "a corner," but not in wheat—
A corner for grandma, a cosy seat,
Away from all doors and winds that blow,
Giving dear grandma the headache so.

We will have it warm, we will have it bright—
Eyes dim with years need unclouded light;
Of access easy to all, but where
The household rush shall not jar her chair.

We would let her choose where the spot shall be,
But too unselfish and meek is she;
I really believe she would choose bare floor,
And crowd herself back by the cellar door.

No, no, Miss Grandma, 'twill never do
To leave your comforts and rights to you:
Your chair shall be covered and soft; your feet
Shall rest on a "cricket," all bright and neat.

You shall sit, and out of the window gaze,
Or on us as we work by the hearth-fire's blaze;
You shall work or be idle, do just as you will—
Hold baby, or not, when he's gentle and still.
The place in this house that is snuggest and best
Is the place we have chosen for dear grandma's rest.

"Why?" Grandma dear, don't you ask us why:
Look at our mother with tearful eye,
Smiling upon you in love untold,
And gratitude not to be purchased with gold

Where had we been, I would like to know,
If grandmother had not so long ago—
When grandpa was far on the stormy main—
Feeble and lonely and often in pain,
So faithfully tended our mother dear
Through years of hardship and little cheer?

You dear old diamond! We understand
The knots and kinks in this little hand:
Indoors and outdoors, and early and late,
You toiled for the sake of your toiling mate—
For the sake of the children you loved so
    well—
And now, like a queen, you shall with them
    dwell.

We all are your subjects, with reverent love,
Delighted to serve you our homage to prove:
Your corner the throne-room, your chair is
    the throne;
Your court is a gay one; your children your
    own,
And your children's children, who round your
    chair
All bless you, and honor your silver hair.
       Augusta Moore, in *The Evangelist*

THE LITTLE YELLOW BEE.

The sun was getting up, and all the hive
    was humming,
There were so many little bees who must be
    taught to roam,
To gather sweetness everywhere, from all the
    blossoms blooming,
And bring their little honey-bags brimful at
    evening home.

Wake up, wake up, young yellow bee! Be
off, the dew is drying;
You must rifle the red clovers, and be early
home to tea;
Now show your graceful swiftness, and your
pretty ways of flying.
For the queen is at the window. and she is
sure to see.

Off flew the little, yellow bee, the fields and
meadows over,
And all the birds' songs in the trees seemed
calling him to play;
There were honeysuckles plenty, and the red
and the white clover;
But he could not tarry toiling such a gladsome summer day.

So he tilted on the grass-blades, and climbed
the tall ferns lightly;
Went swinging in the fox-gloves, and in the
lilies hid;
Played hide and seek with butterflies, and
passed the hours so brightly
That the evening dews were dropping ere he
thought what he was bid.

Oh! the stern queen, and the hive of bees!
how could he ever meet them ?
But it was late, and he was tired, and home
ward he must turn;
Now if, he thought, my honey-bags were full,
then I could greet them
With a low bow, and pardon beg, and thus
my supper earn.

So in the dew and darkness he sought the
sweet white clover,
And filled his little bags so full that he could
hardly fly.

"Who comes so late?" the warder bees cried
  to the weary rover.
"Are you the little loitering drone our queen
  condemns to die?"

He was dragged before her trembling, but
  when he told his story,
Of the bright ecstatic day among the butterflies and birds,
And how he swung on grasses, and kissed a
  morning-glory,
She laughed a merry little laugh, and spoke
  in kindest words.

She wished, she said, her crown were lost, that
  she, too, might go roaming,
Along with bright blue dragon flies, sweet
  gardens down and up;
And then she bade her hive to stop their murmuring and humming,
And ordered bread and honey that the little
  bee might sup.
   Mary L. Bolles Branch,
    in *Youth's Companion*.

WINSOME MAGGIE.

When winsome little Maggie
  Comes dancing down the street,
The people smile upon her,
  And pause, and kindly greet.

The white-haired parson gently
  Lays hand upon her head.
The roguish doctor pinches
  Her cheek so round and red.

The grim old judge's visage,
  Forever in a frown,
Relaxes for an instant,
  As, passing, he looks down.

The matrons stoop to kiss her,
  The children, at their play,
Call out, as little Maggie
  Goes tripping on her way.

Not e'en the dreaded gossip,
  Who through her half-closed blind
Peeps forth, with little Maggie
  Has any fault to find.

When winsome little Maggie,
  With basket on her arm,
In which her father's luncheon
  Is wrapped so nice and warm—

When she enters the long workshop
  And pauses at his side,
Quick down he lays his hammer
  And turns in love and pride,

To look into her limpid eyes,
  And stroke her sunny hair,
And jest and frolic with her—
  Forgetting toil and care—

For the music of her laughter
  And the mirth of her replies,
The while there's not a happier man,
  Or richer, 'neath the skies.

Ah, well, it is a blessing
  To have a heart so gay
That it keeps your feet a-dancing
  Your face alight alway;

And that, like winsome Maggie,
  It seems, where'er you go,
As if the clouds had parted
  To let a sunbeam thro'.
        Ellen Tracy Alden.

"SOMEBODY'S MOTHER."

The woman was old and ragged and gray,
And bent with the chill of a winter's day;
The street was wet with the winter's snow,
And the woman's feet were aged and slow.

She stood at the crossing and waited long,
Alone, uncared for amid a throng

Of human beings, who passed her by,
Nor heeded the glance of her anxious eye.

Down the street, with laughter and shout,
Glad in the freedom of school let out,

Came the boys, like a flock of sheep,
Hailing the snow, piled white and deep.

Past the woman, so old and gray,
Hastened the children on their way,

Nor offered a helping hand to her,
So meek, so timid, afraid to stir,

Lest the carriage wheels or horse's feet
Should crowd her down in the slippery street.

At last came one of the merry troop,
The gayest laddie of all the group.

He paused beside her, and whispered low:
"I'll help you across if you wish to go."

Her aged hand on his strong young arm
She placed, and without hurt or harm

He guided the trembling feet along,
Proud that his own were firm and strong.

Then back again to his friends he went,
His young heart happy and well content.

"She's somebody's mother, boys, you know,
For all she's old and poor and slow,

"And I hope some fellow will lend a hand
To help my mother, you understand,
"If ever she's old and poor and gray;
When her own dear boy is far away."
And "somebody's mother" bowed low her head
In her home that night, and the prayer she said
Was, "God, be kind to the noble boy
Who is somebody's son and pride and joy!"

Home Journal.

WOODMAN, SPARE THAT TREE.

Woodman, spare that tree!
  Touch not a single bough!
In youth it sheltered me,
  And I'll protect it now.
'Twas my forefather's hand
  That placed it near his cot;
There, woodman, let it stand,
  Thy axe shall harm it not!

That old familiar tree,
  Whose glory and renown
Are spread o'er land and sea,
  And wouldst thou hew it down?
Woodman, forebear thy stroke!
  Cut not its earth-bound ties;
O, spare that aged oak,
  Now towering to the skies!

When but an idle boy
  I sought its grateful shade;
In all their gushing joy
  Here too my sisters played.
My mother kissed me here;
  My father pressed my hand—
Forgive this foolish tear,
  But let that old oak stand!

My heart-strings round thee cling,
  Close as thy bark, old friend!
Here shall the wild-bird sing,
  And still thy branches bend,
Old tree! the storm still brave!
  And, woodman, leave that spot;
While I've a hand to save,
  Thy axe shall hurt it not.
                    George P. Morris.

BE HONEST AND TRUE.

BE honest and true,
  O eyes that are blue!
In all that you say
  And all that you do,
If evil you'd shun,
  And good you'd pursue,
If friends you'd have many,
  And foes you'd have few—
Be honest and true
  In all that you say
And all that you do,
  O eyes that are blue!

Be honest and true,
  O eyes that are grey!
In all that you do
  And all that you say
At home or abroad,
  At work or at play,
As you laugh with your friend,
  Or run by the way,
Be honest and true,
  By night and by day,
In all that you do
  And all that you say,
O eyes that are gray!

Be honest and true,
  O eyes that are brown!
On sincerity smile;
  On falsity frown;
All goodness exalt,
  All meanness put down.
As you muse by the fire,
  Or roam through the town,
Remember that honor
  Is manhood's chief crown,
And wear it as yours,
  O eyes that are brown!

Be honest and true,
  O eyes of each hue!—
Brown, black, gray, and blue,
  In all that you say
And all that you do,
  O eyes in which mothers
Look down with delight,
  That sparkle with joy
At things good and bright.
  Do never a thing
You would hide from their sight!
  Stand up for the right
Like a chivalrous knight;
  For the conqueror still,
When the battle is through
  Is he who has ever
Been loyal and true.
  Make the victory sure,
O eyes of each hue!

ONE SATURDAY.

I never had a happier time,
And I am forty-three,
Than one midsummer afternoon,
When it was May with me;

Life's fragrant May,
And Saturday,
And you came up with me to play;
And up and down the garden walks,
Amid the flowering beans,
We proudly walked and tossed our heads,
And played that we were queens!

Thrice prudent sovereigns, we *made*
The diadems we wore,
And fashioned with our royal hands
The sceptres which they bore.
But good Queen Bess
Had surely less
Than we of proud self-consciousness,
While wreaths of honeysuckle hung
Around your rosy neck,
And tufts of marigolds looped up
My gown,—a "gingham check."

Our chosen land was parcelled out,
Like Israel's, by lot.
My kingdom from the garden wall
Reached to the strawberry plot:
The onion bed,
The beet-tops red,
The corn that waved above my head,
The gooseberry-bushes hung with fruit,
The spreading melon-vine,
The carrots and the cabbages,—
All, all of them were mine!

Beneath the cherry-tree was placed
Your throne,—a broken chair;
Your realm was narrower than mine,
But it was twice as fair.
Tall hollyhocks
And purple phlox,
And time-observing "four-o'clocks,"

Blue lavender and candy-tuft,
And pink and white sweet-peas.
Your loyal subjects, waved their heads
In every passing breeze.

O, gayly, prosperously we reigned
Till we were called to tea!
But years, since then, have come and
   gone,
And I am forty-three!
Yet journeying
On restless wing,
Time has not brought, and can not bring,
To you or me a happier hour
Than when, amid the beans,
We proudly walked and tossed our
   heads,
And played that we were queens!
                    Marian Douglas.

THE SEA.

THE sea, the sea, the open sea,
The blue, the fresh, the ever free;
Without a mark, without a bound,
It runneth the earth's wide regions round,
It plays with the clouds, it mocks the skies,
Or like a cradled creature lies.
I'm on the sea, I'm on the sea,
I am where I would ever be,
With the blue above and the blue below,
And silence whereso'er I go,
If a storm should come and awake the deep,
What matter? I shall ride and sleep.

I love, O, how I love to ride
On the fierce, foaming, bursting tide,
Where every mad wave drowns the moon,
And whistles aloft its tempest tune.

And tells how goeth the world below,
And why the southwest wind doth blow!
I never was on the dull, tame shore
But I loved the great sea more and more,
And backward flew to her billowy breast,
Like a bird that seeketh her mother's nest,
And a mother she was and is to me,
For I was born on the open sea.

The waves were white, and red the morn,
In the noisy hour when I was born;
The whale it whistled, the porpoise rolled,
And the dolphins bared their backs of gold;
And never was heard such an outcry wild,
As welcomed to life the ocean child.
I have lived since then, in calm and strife,
Full fifty summers a rover's life,
With wealth to spend, and a power to range,
But never have sought or sighed for change;
And death, whenever he comes to me,
Shall come on the wide, unbounded sea!

Barry Cornwall.

THE BROWN THRUSH.

"There's a merry brown thrush sitting up
    in a tree;
He's singing to me! he's singing to me!"
"And what does he say, little girl, little boy?"
"'Oh, the world's running over with joy!'
    sings he,
  'Don't you hear? Don't you see?
  Hush! look in my tree,
  I'm as happy as happy can be!'"

"And the brown thrush keeps singing, 'A
    nest do you see,
And five eggs hid by me in the juniper-tree?
Don't meddle, don't touch! little girl, little boy,

Or the world will lose some of its joy;
  Now I'm glad! now I'm free!
  And I always shall be,
    If you never bring sorrow to me.'"

"So the merry brown thrush sings away in
    the tree,
To you and to me; to you and to me;
And he sings all the day, little girl, little boy,
'Oh, the world's running over with joy!
    But long it won't be,
    Don't you know? don't you see?
      Unless we're as good as good can be.'"

Lucy Larcom.

THE LITTLE CAVALIER.

He walks beside his mother,
  And looks up in her face;
He wears a glow of boyish pride
  With such a royal grace!
He proudly waits upon her;
  Would shield her without fear—
The boy who loves his mother well,
  Her little cavalier.

To see no tears of sorrow
  Upon her loving cheek,
To gain her sweet approving smile,
  To her to softly speak—
Ah! what in all this wide world
  Could be to him so dear?—
The boy who loves his mother well,
  Her little cavalier.

Look for him in the future
  Among the good, the true:
All blessings on the upward way
  His little feet pursue.

Of robed and crowned and sceptered
    kings
  He stands the royal peer—
The boy who loves his mother well,
  Her little cavalier.
            George Cooper, in *The Nursery*.

THE WIND BLOWS!

HARK!
  The wind blows, and sleet and hail
  Fast follow on the eddying gale—
    The winter seething in the snows:
    The sweeping storm, from height to
      height
    Beats back the huge, devouring night;
  The watchdogs bark
    And the wind blows.

Hark!
  The wind blows, the hills grow brown,
  The snow melts and the rain comes down,
    The swollen current dips and flows;
    The water foams, the bridge gives way;
    By night the horseman drinks the spray;
  The watchdogs bark
    And the wind blows.

Hark!
  The wind blows, the nights grow brief,
  The savage forests burst in leaf,
    The time of planting comes and goes;
    The waters fall, and the sand drifts down;
    Suns pass and no man thinks thereon;
  The watchdogs bark
    And the wind blows.
      Dora Read Goodale, in *Independent*.

A DANISH LEGEND

"Ho, skipper on the sea shore!
    Make ready boat and crew:
Be here to-morrow midnight,
    And you'll have work to do."

The voice was old and feeble:
    The skipper looked around,
And saw a little Troll-man
    Come down from Elleshoi mound.

"I have no boat, good Troll-man,
    Or money one to buy:
My sailors all have left me—
    A luckless man am I."

"Come hither," said the Troll-man,
    And ran along the sand,
To where, on rocks uplifted,
    A battered wreck did stand.

"To-morrow night at midnight
    Come, bring a sailor here:
This vessel shall be ready;
    You have no cause for fear.

"The miller in the village
    Disturbs us night and day:
He ploughs above our houses:
    We can no longer stay.

"The church-bells ring so often,
    We cannot bear their din:
They make us think of heaven,
    Which we can never win."

The little Troll-man vanished;
    The skipper went to ask

A sailor, strong and fearless,
  To help him in the task.

Some laughed at him, some shuddered;
  At last a neighbor's lad
Said, "Take me with you, skipper,
  And I'll fear nothing bad."

At midnight, boy and skipper
  All anchored found the wreck;
For sails, old rags were flapping;
  The Troll was on the deck.

"The wind is fair!" he shouted;
  Make haste to Noroway."
The skipper heaved the anchor;
  The wreck moved down the bay.

The skipper sought the cabin;
  Of rats and mice 'twas full.
"Take this," outspoke the Troll-man,
  And off his hat did pull.

Oh wondrous change! The skipper
  Saw gray-clad, red-capped Trolls,
Who bore upon their shoulders
  Full many a sack of coals.

The wreck was swiftly nearing
  A pine-encircled fiord;
"Go, sailors," said the Troll-man;
  At midnight come on board.

"In three days more be ready
  Just where you found the wreck.
Another cargo waits you;
  You'll find me on the deck."

The skipper took the Troll-folk
  Once more to Noroway.
"Now," said the little Troll-man,
  "You will have earned your pay."

"A sack of coals for master,
  Of shavings for his man;
These are the Troll-folk's presents;
  They give you all they can."

Next morning when the skipper
  Looked down into the hold,
The shavings were all silver—
  The coals were turned to gold.

The skipper's fine new vessel
  Had for its figure-head
A little withered Troll-man,
  Gray-clad, with cap of red.
              Caroline M. Hewins.

THE PIED PIPER OF HAMELIN.

HAMELIN Town's in Brunswick,
By famous Hanover city;
  The river Weser, deep and wide,
  Washes its wall on the southern side,
  A pleasanter spot you never spied;
But when begins my ditty,
  Almost five hundred years ago,
  To see the townsfolk suffer so
From vermin was a pity.

Rats!
They fought the dogs, and killed the cats,
  And bit the babies in their cradles,
And ate the cheeses out of the vats,
  And licked the soup from the cook's own
      ladle,
Split open the kegs of salted sprats,
Made nests inside men's Sunday hats,
And even spoiled the women's chats,
  By drowning their speaking
  With shrieking and squeaking
In fifty different sharps and flats.

At last the people in a body
  To the Town Hall came flocking:
" 'Tis clear," cried they, "our Mayor's a
    noddy;
And as for our Corporation,—shocking
To think we buy gowns lined with ermine
For dolts that can't or won't determine
What's best to rid us of our vermin!"
  At this the Mayor and Corporation
  Quaked with a mighty consternation.

An hour they sat in counsel,—
  At length the Mayor broke silence:
"For a guilder I'd my ermine gown sell;
  I wish I were a mile hence!
It's easy to bid one rack one's brain,—
I'm sure my poor head aches again
I've scratched it so and all in vain.
  O for a trap, a trap, a trap!"
Just as he said this, what should hap
At the chamber door but a gentle tap!
"Bless us," cried the Mayor, "what's that?"
"Come in!" the Mayor cried looking bigger,
And in did come the strangest figure;
He advanced to the council-table
And, "Please your honors," said he, "I'm
    able,
By means of a secret charm, to draw
All creatures living beneath the sun,
That creep or swim or fly or run,
After me so as you never saw!
"Yet," said he, "poor piper as I am,
In Tartary I freed the Cham,
Last June, from his huge swarm of gnats;
I eased in Asia the Nizam
Of a monstrous brood of vampire-bats;—
And as for what your brain bewilders,—
If I can rid your town of rats,
Will you give me a thousand guilders?"
"One? fifty thousand!"—was the exclamation
Of the astonished Mayor and Corporation.

Into the street the piper stept
  Smiling first a little smile,
As if he knew what magic slept
  In his quiet pipe the while;
Then, like a musical adept,
To blow the pipe his lips he wrinkled,
And green and blue his sharp eyes twinkled,
Like a candle flame where salt is sprinkled;
And ere three shrill notes the pipe uttered,
You heard as if an army muttered;
And the muttering grew to a grumbling;
And the grumbling grew to a mighty rumbling;
And out of the houses the rats came tumbling.
Great rats, small rats, lean rats, brawny rats,
Brown rats, black rats, grey rats, tawny rats,
Grave old plodders, gay young friskers,
  Fathers, mothers, uncles, cousins,
Cocking tails and pricking whiskers;
  Families by tens and dozens,
Brothers, sisters, husbands, wives,—
Followed the piper for their lives.
From street to street he piped advancing,
And step for step they followed dancing,
Until they came to the river Weser,
Wherein all plunged and perished
Save one who, stout as Julius Cæsar,
Swam across and lived to carry
(As he the manuscript he cherished)
To Rat-land home his commentary,
Which was: "At the first shrill notes of the
    pipe,
I heard a sound as of scraping tripe,
And putting apples, wondrous ripe,
Into a cider-press's gripe,—
And a moving away of pickle-tub boards,
And a leaving ajar of conserve-cupboards,
And a drawing the corks of train-oil flasks,
And a breaking the hoops of butter-casks;
And it seemed as if a voice
(Sweeter far than by harp or by psaltery

Is breathed) called out, O rats, rejoice!
The world is grown to one vast drysaltery!
So munch on, crunch on, take your muncheon,
Breakfast, supper, dinner, luncheon!
And just as a bulky sugar puncheon,
All ready staved, like a great sun shone
Glorious scarce an inch before me,
Just as methought it said, Come bore me!
I found the Weser rolling o'er me."

You should have heard the Hamelin people
Ringing the bells till they rocked the steeple;
"Go," cried the Mayor, "and get long poles!
Poke out the nests and block up the holes!
Consult with carpenters and builders
And leave in our town not even a trace
Of the rats!"—when suddenly, up the face
Of the piper perked in the market-place,
With a "First if you please, my thousand guilders!"

A thousand guilders! the Mayor looked blue;
So did the Corporation too.
For council-dinners made rare havock
With Claret, Moselle, Vin-de-Grave, Hock;
And half the money would replenish
Their cellar's biggest butt with Rhenish,
To pay this sum to a wandering fellow
With a gypsy coat of red and yellow!
"Beside," quoth the Mayor, with a knowing wink,
"Our business was done at the river's brink;
We saw with our eyes the vermin sink,
And what's dead can't come to life I think,
So, friend, we're not the folks to shrink
From the duty of giving you something for drink,
And a matter of money to put in you poke;
But as for the guilders, what we spoke
Of them, as you very well know, was in joke.

Besides, our losses have made us thrifty;
A thousand guilders! Come, take fifty."

The piper's face fell, and he cried,
"No trifling! I can't wait! beside,
I've promised to visit by dinner time
Bagdat, and accept the prime
Of the head-cook's pottage, all he's rich in,
For having left, in the Caliph's kitchen,
Of a nest of scorpions no survivor,—
With him I proved no bargain-driver;
With you, don't think I'll bate a stiver!
And folks who put me in a passion
May find me pipe another fashion."

"How?" cried the Mayor, "d'ye think I'll brook
Being worse treated than a cook?
Insulted by a lazy ribald
With idle pipe and vesture piebald?
You threaten us, fellow? Do your worst,
Blow your pipe there till you burst!"

Once more he stept into the street;
  And to his lips again
Laid his long pipe of smooth straight cane;
  And ere he blew three notes (such sweet
Soft notes as yet musician's cunning
  Never gave the enraptured air)
There was a rustling that seemed like a bustling
Of merry crowds justling at pitching and hustling;
Small feet were pattering, wooden shoes clattering,
Little hands clapping, and little tongues chattering;
And, like fowls in a farm-yard when barley is scattering,
Out came the children running;

All the little boys and girls,
With rosy cheeks and flaxen curls,
And sparkling eyes and teeth like pearls,
Tripping and skipping, ran merrily after
The wonderful music with shouting and
   laughter.

The Mayor was dumb, and the Council stood
As if they were changed into blocks of wood;
Unable to move a step, or cry
To the children merrily skipping by,—
And could only follow with the eye
That joyous crowd at the piper's beck.
But how the Mayor was on the rack,
And the wretched Council's bosoms beat,
As the piper turned from the High Street
To where the Weser rolled its waters
Right in the way of their sons and daughters!
However, he turned from south to west,
And to Koppelberg Hill his steps addressed,
And after him the children pressed;
Great was the joy in every breast.
"He never can cross that mighty top!
He's forced to let the piping drop,
And we shall see our children stop!"
When, lo, as they reached the mountain's side,
A wondrous portal opened wide,
As if a cavern was suddenly hollowed;
And the piper advanced and the children
   followed;
And when all were in, to the very last,
The door in the mountain-side shut fast.
Did I say all? No! One was lame,
And could not dance the whole of the way;
And in after years, if you would blame
His sadness, he was used to say,—
"It's dull in our town since my playmates left!
I can't forget that I'm bereft
Of all the pleasant sights they see,

Which the piper also promised me:
For he led us, he said, to a joyous land,
Joining the town, and just at hand,
Where waters gushed and fruit-trees grew,
And flowers put forth a fairer hue,
And everything was strange and new;
The sparrows were brighter than peacocks here,
And their dogs outran their fallow deer,
And honey-bees had lost their stings,
And horses were born with eagle's wings;
And just as I became assured
My lame foot would be speedily cured,
The music stopped and I stood still,
And found myself outside the Hill,
Left alone against my will,
To go now limping as before,
And never hear of that country more!"
Robert Browning.

THE SPIDER AND THE FLY.

"Will you walk into my parlor?"
 Said a spider to a fly;
"'Tis the prettiest little parlor
 That ever you did spy.
The way into my parlor
 Is up a winding stair,
And I have many pretty things
 To show you when you're there."
"Oh no, no!" said the little fly;
 "To ask me is in vain;
For who goes up your winding stair
 Can ne'er come down again."

"I'm sure you must be weary
 With soaring up so high;
Will you rest upon my little bed?"
 Said the spider to the fly.

" There are pretty curtains drawn around,
  The sheets are fine and thin,
And if you like to rest awhile,
  I'll snugly tuck you in."
" Oh no, no!" said the little fly,
  " For I've often heard it said
They never never wake again
  Who sleep upon your bed."

Said the cunning spider to the fly,
  " Dear friend, what shall I do
To prove the warm affection
  I've always felt for you?
I have within my pantry
  Good store of all that's nice;
I'm sure you're very welcome—
  Will you please to take a slice?"
" Oh no, no!" said the little fly;
  " Kind sir, that cannot be;
I've heard what's in your pantry,
  And I do not wish to see."

"Sweet creature," said the spider,
  " You're witty and your wise:
How handsome are your gauzy wings!
  How brilliant are your eyes!
I have a little looking-glass
  Upon my parlor shelf:
If you'll step in one moment, dear,
  You shall behold yourself."
" I thank you, gentle sir," she said,
  " For what you're pleased to say;
And, bidding you good-morning now,
  I'll call another day."

The spider turned him round about,
  And went into his den,
For well he knew the silly fly
  Would soon be back again;
So he wove a subtle thread

In a little corner sly,
And set his table ready
  To dine upon the fly.
He went out to his door again,
  And merrily did sing,
"Come hither, hither, pretty fly,
  With pearl and silver wing!
Your robes are green and purple
  There's a crest upon your head!
Your eyes are like the diamonds bright,
  But mine are dull as lead."

Alas! alas! how very soon
  This silly little fly.
Hearing his wily, flattering words,
  Came slowly flitting by:
With buzzing wings she hung aloft,
  Then near and nearer drew—
Thought only of her brilliant eyes
  And green and purple hue:
Thought only of her crested head—
  Poor foolish thing! At last
Up jumped the cunning spider,
  And fiercely held her fast.

He dragged her up his winding stair,
  Into his dismal den
Within his little parlor—but
  She ne'er came out again!
And now, dear little children,
  Who may this story read.
To idle, silly, flattering words
  I pray you ne'er give heed.
Unto an evil counsellor
    Close heart, and ear, and eye,
And learn a lesson from this tale
  Of the spider and the fly.
            Mary Howitt.

THE WISE FAIRY.

Once, in a rough, wild country,
  On the other side of the sea,
There lived a dear little fairy,
  And her home was in a tree.
A dear little queer little fairy,
  And as rich as she could be.

To northward and to southward,
  She could overlook the land,
And that was why she had her house
  In a tree, you understand.
For she was the friend of the friendless
  And her heart was in her hand.

And when she saw poor women
  Patiently, day by day,
Spinning, spinning, and spinning
  Their lonesome lives away,
She would hide in the flax of their distaffs
  A lump of gold, they say.

And when she saw poor ditchers
  Knee-deep in some wet dyke,
Digging, digging, and digging,
  To their very graves, belike,
She would hide a shining lump of gold
  Where their spades would be sure to
    strike.

And when she saw poor children
  Their goats from the pastures take,
Or saw them milking and milking,
  Till their arms were ready to break,
What a plashing in their milking-pails
  Her gifts of gold would make!

Sometimes in the night, a fisher
 Would hear her sweet low call,
And all at once a salmon of gold
 Right out of his net would fall;
But what I have to tell you
 Is the strangest thing of all.

If any ditcher, or fisher,
 Or child, or spinner old,
Bought shoes for his feet, or bread to eat,
 Or a coat to keep from the cold,
The gift of the good old fairy
 Was always trusty gold.

But if a ditcher, or fisher,
 Or spinner, or child so gay,
Bought jewels. or wine, or silks so fine,
 Or staked his pleasure at play,
The fairy's gold in his very hold
 Would turn to a lump of clay.

So, by and by the people
 Got open their stupid eyes:
"We must learn to spend to some good
  end,"
They said, "if we are wise;
'Tis not in the gold we waste or hold,
 That a golden blessing lies."
                         Alice Cary.

THE DEATH OF THE FLOWERS.

THE melancholy days are come, the saddest
 of the year,
Of wailing winds, and naked woods, and
 meadows brown and sere,
Heaped in the hollows of the grove, the
 autumn leaves lie dead:

They rustle to the eddying gust, and to the
    rabbit's tread;
The robin and the wren are flown, and from
    the shrubs the jay,
And from the wood-top calls the crow,
    through all the gloomy day.

Where are the flowers, the fair young flowers,
    that lately sprung and stood
In brighter light and softer airs, a beauteous
    sisterhood?
Alas! they all are in their graves, the gentle
    race of flowers
Are lying in their lowly beds, with the fair
    and good of ours.
The rain is falling where they lie; but the
    cold November rain
Calls not, from out the gloomy earth, the
    lovely ones again.

The wind-flower and the violet, they perished
    long ago,
And the brier-rose and the orchis died amid
    the summer's glow;
But on the hill the golden-rod, and the aster
    in the wood.
And the yellow sunflower by the brook in
    autumn beauty stood,
Till fell the frost from the clear, cold heaven,
    as falls the plague on men,
And the brightness of their smile was gone
    from upland, glade and glen.

And now when comes the calm, mild day, as
    still such days will come,
To call the squirrel and the bee from out their
    winter home,
When the sound of dropping nuts is heard,
    though all the trees are still,
And twinkle in the smoky light the waters of
    the rill,

The south-wind searches for the flowers whose
    fragrance late he bore,
And sighs to find them in the wood and by
    the stream no more.

And then I think of one who in her youthful
    beauty died,
The fair, meek blossom that grew up and
    faded by my side:
In the cold moist earth we laid her when the
    forest cast the leaf,
And we wept that one so lovely should have
    a life so brief;
Yet not unmeet it was, that one, like that
    young friend of ours
So gentle and so beautiful, should perish with
    the flowers.
William Cullen Bryant.

THE SECRET OF A HAPPY DAY.

Just to let thy father do
    What He will;
Just to know that He is true
    And be still.
Just to follow hour by hour
    As He leadeth;
Just to draw the moment's power
    As it needeth.
Just to trust Him, this is all!
    Then the day will surely be
Peaceful, whatsoe'er befall,
    Bright and blessed, calm and free.

Just to let Him speak to thee
    Through His Word,
Watching, that His voice may be
    Clearly heard.
Just to tell Him everything

As it rises,
And at once to Him to bring
All surprises.
Just to listen, and to stay
Where you cannot miss His voice.
This is all! and thus to-day,
Communing, you shall rejoice.

Just to trust, and yet to ask
Guidance still;
Take the training or the task,
As He will.
Just to take the loss or gain,
As He sends it;
Just to take the joy or pain,
As He lends it.
He who formed thee for His praise
Will not miss the gracious aim;
So to-day and all thy days
Shall be moulded for the same.

Just to leave in His dear hand
Little things
All we cannot understand,
All that stings.
Just to let Him take the care
Sorely pressing,
Finding all we let Him bear
Changed to blessing.
This is all! and yet the way
Marked by Him who loves thee best;
Secret of a happy day,
Secret of His promised rest.

Frances Ridley Havergal.

THE COLOR BEARER.

'Twas a fortress to be stormed;
Boldly right in view they formed,
All as quiet as a regiment parading:
Then in front a line of flame!
Then at left and right the same!
Two platoons received a furious enfilading
To their places still they filed,
And they smiled at the wild
  Cannonading.

" 'Twill be over in an hour!
'Twill not be much of a shower!
Never mind, my boys," said he, "a little
    drizzling!"
Then to cross that fatal plain,
Through the whirring, hustling rain
Of the grape-shot, and the minie-bullets'
    whistling.
But he nothing heeds nor shuns,
As he runs with the guns
  Brightly bristling!

Over tangled branches crashing,
'Mid the plunging volleys thundering
    ever louder!
There he clambers, there he stands,
With the ensign in his hands,—
O, was ever hero handsomer or prouder?
Streaked with battle-sweat and slime,
And sublime in the grime
  Of the powder!

'Twas six minutes, at the least,
Ere the closing combat ceased,—
Near as we the mighty moments then
  could measure,—

And we held our souls with awe,
Till his haughty flag we saw
On the lifting vapors drifting o'er the
    embrasure!
Saw it glimmer in our tears,
While our ears heard the cheers
    Rend the azure!

Through the abatis they broke,
Leaving trails of dead and dying
In their track, yet forward flying
Like a breaker where the gale of conflict
    rolled them,
With a foam of flashing light
Borne before them on their bright
Burnished barrels,—O, 't was fearful to
    behold them!
While from ramparts roaring loud
Swept a cloud like a shroud
    To enfold them!

O, his color was the first!
Through the burying cloud he burst,
With the standard to the battle forward
    slanted!
Through the belching, blinding breath
Of the flaming jaws of Death,
Till his banner on the bastion he had
    planted!
By the screaming shot that fell,
And the yell of the shell,
    Nothing daunted.

Right against the bulwark dashing,
Through the surging cannon-smoke,
And they drove the foe before like
    frightened cattle!
O, but never wound was his,
For in other wars than this
When the volleys of Life's conflict roar
    and rattle,

He must still, as he was wont,
In the front bear the brunt
    Of the battle.

He shall guide the van of Truth!
And in manhood, as in youth,
Be her fearless, be her peerless Color-
    Bearer!
With his high and bright example,
Like a banner brave and ample,
Ever leading through receding clouds of
    Error,
To the empire of the Strong.
And to Wrong he shall long
    Be a terror!
            J. T. Trowbridge.

DAY-DREAMS.

WHILE the slighted grammar unopened lay,
    The little maid dreamed of a fairy clue,
A magic thread that led far and away
    The deep, tangled maze of the forest through;

"O! I wish there were things to do to-day,
    Queer riddles to solve, great prizes to gain,
Enchantments to break, magicians to slay,
    And that I, a queen, on a throne might
        reign!

"But the puzzles are lost, the queens are
        dead,
    And there's nothing to do," she sighed
        and said.

A little lad leaned on his hoe that morn,
    And longed for a horse and a burnished
        shield,
To ride away from the pumpkins and corn,
    To the tourney's lists on the tented field;—

"O! I wish there were things to do to-day,
  Great dragons to kill and battles to fight;
I would break a lance in the fiercest fray,
  I would fling a glove at the proudest knight.

"But honor is lost, and glory has fled,
  And there's nothing to do," he sighed and said.

And the poor little maiden never knew
  That Knowledge was ready to crown her queen,
And the clue that led his labyrinth through
  Lay hidden the leaves of her book between.

And the little lad never even guessed
  That the dragon Sloth conquered him that day,
While he lightly dreamed of some idle quest,
  And his unused hoe in the young corn lay.

But honor and fame passed the dreamers by,
  And crowned brave Toil, who found no time to sigh.
            Annie M. Libby, in S. S. Times.

THE BROOK THAT RAN INTO THE SEA.

"O LITTLE brook," the children said,
  The sea has waves enough;
Why hurry down your mossy bed
  To meet his welcome rough?

"The Hudson or the Oregon
  May help his tides to swell;
But when your few bright drops are gone,
  What has he gained, pray tell?"

"I run for pleasure," said the brook,
　　Still running, running fast:
"I love to see you bend and look,
　　As I go bubbling past.

"I love to feel the wild weeds dip;
　　I love your fingers light,
That dimpling from my eddies drip,
　　Filled with my pebbles bright.

"My little life I dearly love,
　　Its shadow and its shine ;
And all sweet voices that above
　　Make melody with mine.

"But most I love the mighty voice
　　Which calls me, draws me so,
That every ripple lisps. 'Rejoice!'
　　As with a laugh I go.

"My drop of freshness to the sea
　　In music trickles on ;
Nor grander could my welcome be
　　Were I an Amazon.

"And if his moaning wave can feel
　　My sweetness near the shore,
E'en to his heart the thrill may steal:—
　　What could I wish for. more ?

"The largest soul to take love in
　　Knows how to give love best;
So peacefully my tinkling din
　　Dies on the great sea's breast.

"One heart encircles all that live.
　　And blesses great and small;
And meet it is that each should give
　　His little to the All."

　　　　　　　　　　Lucy Larcom.

WORK.

Sweet wind, fair wind, where have you been?
"I've been sweeping the cobwebs out of the
 sky;
I've been grinding a grist in the mill hard by;
I've been laughing at work while others sigh;
 Let those laugh who win!"

Sweet rain, soft rain, what are you doing?
"I'm urging the corn to fill out its cells;
I'm helping the lily to fashion its bells;
I'm swelling the torrent and brimming the
 wells;
 Is that worth pursuing?"

Redbreast, redbreast, what have you done?
"I've been watching the nest where my
 fledglings lie;
I've sung them to sleep with a lullaby;
By and by I shall teach them to fly,
 Up and away every one!"

Honey-bee, honey-bee, where are you going?
"To fill my basket with precious pelf;
To toil for my neighbor as well as myself;
To find out the sweetest flower that grows,
Be it a thistle or be it a rose,—
 A secret worth the knowing!"

Each content with the work to be done,
Ever the same from sun to sun:
Shall you and I be taught to work
By the bee and the bird that scorn to shirk?

Wind and rain fulfilling His word!
Tell me, was ever a legend heard
Where the wind, commanded to blow deferred;
Or the rain, that was bidden to fall demurred?
 Mary N. Prescott.

BEFORE SNOW-TIME.

THE buttercups out of the meadows go,
    Hippity, hippity, hop!
The chicory-flowers no longer blow,
For away way off do they smell the snow
That will bury them deeply if they stop,
    So hippity, hippity, hop!

The cattle come up to the shed right soon,
    Hippity, hippity, hop!
For well do they know 'tis a rainy moon,
And they hear no longer the bull-frog's croon,
So in they come to the barn-stored crop;
    Hippity, hippity, hop!

Now two little children so blithe and so good,
    Hippity, hippity, hop!
Drawn close 'round the fire of hickory wood,
(While mother sits knitting a pretty blue hood,)
With apples for roasting and red corn to pop,
    Hippity, hippity, hop!

Then laugh and be merry though summer has fled,
    Hippity, hippity, hop!
And tree-leaves are brown that were golden and red,
And even the asters have crept into bed:—
O let us laugh loud as we hear the rain drop,
    Hippity, hippity, hop!
    James Berry Bensel,
        in *Our Little Men and Women.*

LIGHT FOR ALL.

Jesus bids us shine
  With a clear pure light,
Like a little candle
  Burning in the night.
All the world is dark,
  So we must shine;
You in your small corner,
  And I in mine.

Jesus bids us shine,
  First of all for Him;
Well He sees and knows it
  If our light is dim.
He looks down from Heaven,
  To see us shine;
You in your small corner,
  And I in mine.

Jesus bids us shine!
  When we look around,
Oh, what depths of darkness
  In the world are found.
There's sin, there's want, there's
    sorrow,
  So we must shine;
You in your small corner,
  And I in mine.
                    S. S. Advocate.

A VISIT FROM ST. NICHOLAS.

'Twas the night before Christmas, when all through the house,
Not a creature was stirring, not even a mouse;
The stockings were hung by the chimney with care,
In hopes that St. Nicholas soon would be there;
The children were nestled all snug in their beds,
While visions of sugar-plums danced in their heads;
And mamma in her 'kerchief, and I in my cap,
Had just settled our brains for a long winter's nap,
When out on the lawn there arose such a clatter
I sprang from my bed to see what was the matter.
Away to the window I flew like a flash,
Tore open the shutters and threw up the sash.
The moon, on the breast of the new-fallen snow
Gave a lustre of midday to objects below.
When what to my wondering eyes should appear
But a miniature sleigh, and eight tiny reindeer,
With a little old driver, so lively and quick,
I knew in a moment it must be St. Nick.
More rapid than eagles his coursers they came,
And he whistled, and shouted, and called them by name:

"Now, Dasher! now, Dancer! now Prancer, and Vixen!
On, Comet! on, Cupid! on Donder and Blitzen!
To the top of the porch! to the top of the wall!
Now dash away! dash away! dash away all!
As dry leaves that before the wild hurricane fly,
When they meet with an obstacle mount to the sky,
So up to the house-top the coursers they flew,
With the sleigh full of toys, and St. Nicholas too.
And then, in a twinkling, I heard on the roof
The prancing and pawing of each little hoof;
As I drew in my head and was turning around,
Down the chimney St. Nicholas came with a bound.
He was dressed all in fur from his head to his foot,
And his clothes were all tarnished with ashes and soot;
A bundle of toys he had flung on his back,
And he looked like a peddler just opening his pack.
His eyes—how they twinkled! his dimples how merry!
His cheeks were like roses, his nose like a cherry!
His droll little mouth was drawn up like a bow,
And the beard on his chin was as white as the snow;
The stump of a pipe he held tight in his teeth,
And the smoke it encircled his head like a wreath.
He was chubby and plump, a right jolly old elf;
And I laughed when I saw him in spite of myself;
A wink of his eye, and a twist of his head,

Soon gave me to know I had nothing to dread.
He spoke not a word, but went straight to his work,
And filled all the stockings; then turned with a jerk,
And laying his finger aside of his nose,
And giving a nod, up the chimney he rose.
He sprung to his sleigh, to his team gave a whistle,
And away they all flew like the down of a thistle.
But I heard him exclaim, as he drove out of sight,
"Merry Christmas to all! and to all a good-night!"

Clement C. Moore.

A DINNER AND A KISS.

"I HAVE brought your dinner, father,"
   The blacksmith's daughter said,
As she took from her arm the kettle,
   And lifted its steaming lid.
"There is not any pie or pudding:
   So I will give you this;"
And upon his toil-worn forehead
   She left a childish kiss.

The blacksmith took off his apron,
   And dined in a happy mood,
Wondering much at the savor
   Hid in his humble food,
While all about him were visions
   Full of prophetic bliss;
But he never thought of the magic
   In his little daughter's kiss.

While she, with her kettle swinging,
   Merrily trudged away,

Stopping at sight of a squirrel,
   Catching some wild bird's lay.
O, I thought, how many a shadow
   Of life and fate we would miss,
If always our frugal dinners
   Were seasoned with a kiss!

THE ANGEL'S BLESSING.

A MINISTERING Angel
   Just at the edge of even,
Was flying slowly earthward
   With messages from Heaven.
A peaceful golden sunset
   Was brightening the west
And happy little children
   Were going to their rest.

The Angel paused and listened
   As on the evening air,
Rose mingled mother-blessing
   And childhood's guileless prayer;
And softly from his pinions
   He wafted slumbers deep
Upon their happy eyelids,
   And gave them dreamless sleep.

But then almost a shadow
   Across his brightness swept,
As rose the mournful voices
   Of little ones who wept;
Pale babes of want and sorrow,
   Bereft of mother-care,
Who, orphaned or forsaken,
   Had only tears for prayer.

The ministering Angel
   No longer stayed his flight,
But to the weeping children

He sped on wings of light.
And while they thought his glories
Were but the sunset gleams,
He kissed their tearful eyelids,
And gave them happy dreams.
Amelia Daley Alden.

THE ANGEL'S SONG.

It came upon the midnight clear,
That glorious song of old.
From angels bending near the earth
To touch their harps of gold.
"Peace on the earth, good-will to men."
From Heaven's all gracious king;
The world in solemn stillness lay
To hear the angels sing.

Still through the cloven skies they came
With peaceful wings unfurled:
And still their heavenly music floats
O'er all the weary world:
Above its sad and lowly plains
They bend on hovering wing,
And ever o'er its Babel sounds
The blessed angels sing.

But with the woes of sin and strife
The world has suffered long;
Beneath the angel-strain have rolled
Two thousand years of wrong;
And man at war with man, hears not
The love-song which they bring:
Oh! hush the noise, ye men of strife,
And hear the angels sing!

And ye, beneath life's crushing load
Whose forms are bending low,
Who toil along the climbing way
With painful steps and slow;

Look now! for glad and golden hours
  Come swiftly on the wing;
Oh! rest beside the weary road,
  And hear the angels sing!

For lo! the days are hastening on,
  By prophet bards foretold;
When with the ever-circling years
  Comes round the age of gold;
When peace shall over all the earth
  Its ancient splendors fling,
And the whole world send back the song
  Which now the angels sing.
           Edmund H. Sears.

A CHRISTMAS CAROL.

I.

COME forth, ye wandering children all,
  Come forth from wood and wild,
And let us sing the days of Christ,
  When He was but a child.

When He was but a little child,
  As tender as might be;
That blessed night pale Mary came
  From distant Galilee.

That night, when 'mid the cattle herd,
  Pure as the snow that falls,
The voice that breathed our Father's love,
  Was hushed among the stalls.

It was the dreary winter-tide,
  And dark the hour He came;
But such a brightness round him burned,
  The east was all a-flame.

He made a wonder where He lay;
  Quickened with love and fear,
The barren straw did swell with grain
  Ripe in the fruitful ear.

All round this shed the frozen bees
  Went singing, singing sweet;
The lowly herd, bowed down with fear,
  Fell kneeling at His feet.

And Mary, on her sleeping Son,
  In solemn gladness smiled;
Remember! 'twas the sacred time
  When Christ was but a child.

II.

He came to shew the waters pure
  Where thirsting souls might sip;
The bread of life was on His tongue,
  Its wine upon His lip.

The sages cast before His feet
  Their jewels. costly-rare;
Those feet which late had trod the skies,
  Where all His riches were.

They held a crown above His head,
  With gems all bristled o'er;
It might have been a crown of thorns
  That pressed and pierced Him sore.

It stirred Him from His slumbers calm;
  A change passed o'er His sleep;
Though yet no healing word He spoke,
  His sighs came long and deep.

And ever on His heaving breast,
  By troubled visions tossed,
Still folded in a mystic sign,
  His tender arms He crossed.

Though Mary-mother undid the clasp,
 Her care it was but loss;
For still the silent sleeper's arms
 Would form that mystic cross.

It might not be a thing of chance,
 Nor empty vision wild;
Remember! 'twas the wonderous time
 When Christ was but a child.

III.

The daylight dawned, and Jesus woke,
 And gazed upon His mother;
Then, searching wide with anxious eyes,
 He seemed to seek Another.

He might not weep as children weep,
 But, on her bosom leaning,
With speaking looks He clung to her,
 With looks of mournful meaning.

His lips, at her half-uttered prayer,
 Were moved, but made no moan;
Her holy eyes, upturned to heaven,
 He followed with His own.

And steps came in, and steps went out,
 That passed not by the door;
And a dreary shadow stole along,
 And fell upon the floor.

And a voice, like that on Calvary,
 Rang through the frozen air,
In the anguish of the crucified;
 The passion, and the prayer.

Then slow the wintry winds died down,
 Hushed was the herd's low bleating;
No sound was heard in that lone shed,
 Only their two hearts beating.

So found He safety on the breast
Of Mary-mother mild;
Remember! 'twas the hallowed time
When Christ was but a child.
Mrs. J. K. Hervey.

CHRISTMAS.

How shall I tell of the ages,
  When Christmas was never kept;
When the earth, in dark revolution,
  Bided her time—and slept ?
How speak of the tardy unfolding
  Of morn in the crimson East—
When lo! for the heavenly infant
  There waited the solemn feast?
    The Shepherds sing
      In slow accord,
    "Is born our King,
      The blessed Lord."

A quiver—as if down the ages
  Mortality's cry echoed still;
So long had it voiced every heart-beat,
  It lingered the daybreak to fill;
Each bitter, discordant, low earth-wail
  Shocked heavenly air as it rang;
The Babe breathed; Divinity woke,
  And the Angels in rapture sang.
    The Shepherds say,
      "We seek Him, all.
    Look at the Star
      O'er Bethlehem's stall."

The Babe enwrapped in the manger,
  His tiny hand folded soft;
That hand, to be put forth for others
  In loving strength, so oft;
To be, even in willing submission,

Extended from Calvary,
Now rests on the Mother's bosom,
In beautiful infancy.
  The Shepherds whisper,
   On each knee,
 " *We bring our gifts,*
  O Lord, to Thee."

That head on its pillow so tender,
Must wear a thorny crown,
Before, the earth-life ended,
Its sacrifice lays down;
But now, oh! gracious promise
Of kingly power and might,
It sends out from the little brow
Rays of divinest light.
  The Shepherds veil
   Their faces now;
 "To thee, O Lord,
  We humbly bow."

Oh! now the pæans rolling,
 The anthems meet and blend;
"Give praises, oh! give praises,
 Forever, without end."
"The Christchild ne'er shall leave us,"
 The angels soft do sing;
"But always folded in our hearts,
 The Christmas joy shall bring."
  The Shepherds then
   Stole soft away,
 "The night has flown,
  Look! break of day."

What does it mean, this Christmas,
 Down from the ages sent?
Out of the lips of a little child,
 What is the message meant?
Into one word it is prisoned,
 Struck into life and light;

Love is the Christmas-tide message
Of heavenly power and might.
The Shepherds far
Upon the plain,
Adore the Lord
Of Love again.

Sing it in heavenly chorus,
Sing it in earthly strain,
Wake the dark places with music,
To call down the Lord again.
Sing it 'mid Christmas jangle
Of bell and childish voice,
And sweet confusion, sing it:
"*Our Lord is come! Rejoice!*"
The Christmas bells
O'er hill and plain,
Take up the Shepherds'
Sweet refrain:
"The child is born
To bring us Love
And Light and Peace
From God above."
Margaret Sidney, in *Independent.*

LITTLE BY LITTLE.

LITTLE by little the time goes by—
Short if you sing through it, long if you sigh;
Little by little—an hour, a day,
Gone with the years that have vanished away;
Little by little the race is run,
Trouble and waiting and toil are done!
Little by little the world grows strong,
Fighting the battles of right and wrong;
Little by little the wrong gives way,
Little by little right has sway;
Little by little all longing souls
Struggle up nearer the shining goals.
Youth's Companion.

OLD CHRISTMAS.

Now he who knows old Christmas,
  He knows a carle of worth;
For he is as good a fellow
  As any upon earth.

He comes warm cloaked and coated,
  And buttoned up to the chin,
And soon as he comes anigh the door
  We open and let him in.

We know that he will not fail us,
  So we sweep the hearth up clean;
We set him in the old arm-chair,
  And a cushion whereon to lean;

And with sprigs of holly and ivy
  We make the house look gay,
Just out of an old regard for him,
  For it was his ancient way.

We broach the strong ale-barrel,
  And bring out wine and meat;
And thus have all things ready
  Our dear old friend to greet.

And soon the time wears round;
  The good old carle we see
Coming anear, for a creditor
  Less punctual is than he.

He comes with a cordial voice,
  That does one good to hear;
He shakes one heartily by the hand,
  As he hath done many a year.

And after the little children
  He asks in a cheerful tone—

Jack, Kate, and little Annie;
He remembers every one.

What a fine old fellow he is,
With his faculties all as clear,
And his heart as warm and light,
As a man in his fortieth year!

What a fine old fellow, in troth!
Not one of your griping elves,
Who, with plenty of money to spare,
Think only about themselves.

Not he! for he loveth the children,
And holiday begs for all;
And comes with his pockets full of gifts
For the great ones and the small.

And he tells us witty old stories,
And singeth with might and main;
And we talk of the old man's visit
Till the day that he comes again.

Oh, he is a kind old fellow,
For, though the beef is dear,
He giveth the parish paupers
A good dinner once a year.

And all the workhouse children
He sets them down in a row,
And giveth them rare plum-pudding,
And twopence apiece also.

Oh, could you have seen those paupers,
Have heard those children young,
You would wish with them that Christmas
Came oft and tarried long.

He must be a rich old fellow;
What money he gives away!

There's not a lord in England
 Could equal him any day.

Good luck unto Old Christmas,
 And long life, let us sing!
For he doth more good unto the poor
 Than many a crowned king
                    Mary Howitt.

AN OLD LEGEND.

THE snow came falling fast and fair
 Down through the dreary night;
The Christmas lights shone everywhere,
 The city streets were bright;
And loud the sweet cathedral bells
 Chimed praises and delight.

But out amid the falling snow,
 Forsaken and alone,
A little child went wandering slow
 And making piteous moan;
For his father and his mother dear
 Up into heaven were gone.

He saw the fruitful Christmas-trees
 Spread out their gracious boughs;
He saw between the curtains red
 The children's shining brows,
And the little Christ-child sitting high
 To hear their thankful vows.

Then loud he cried, and sobbed full sore;
 No mother dear had he
To fill his apron from her store,
 And take him on her knee.
He cried till a rich woman heard,
 And came outside to see.

"O lady! give me fire and food,
    I am so starved and cold,
Please do the little orphan good,
    For God has sent you gold!"
But she said, "Begone, thou beggar boy!
    My house no more can hold."

She shut him out into the night,
    And went among her own;
She sat upon a cushion bright,
    He on the stepping stone,
And his tears made little drops of ice
    As he sat there alone.

But down the wide and snowy street
    He saw another child,
With silver sandals on his feet,
    Float through the tempest wild,
His snow-white garments shining fair,
    As if a sunbeam smiled.

Right onward to the orphan lad
    Down the wide street he came,
And in a voice full sweet and glad
    He called him by his name,
And the little weary child grew warm,
    Forgetting pain and shame.

"Thou hast no home, thou little one,
    But thou shalt go with me;
I saw thee sitting all alone,
    And I came after thee.
Now look up to the heavens above,
    Behold thy Christmas tree!"

The boy looked up to heaven above,
    His tears forgot to flow;
For the Christ-child with his looks of love
    Had charmed away the snow,
And on a tree all set with stars
    Angels went to and fro.

"Come up! come up, thou little boy!
Come up to heaven on high!
Thy Christmas-tide shall dawn in joy."
He clasped him lovingly,
And the Christ-child and the orphan lad
Kept Christmas in the sky.
   Rose Terry, in *Our Young Folks.*

THE THREE KINGS.

THREE kings came riding from far away,
 Melchior and Gasper and Baltazar;
Three Wise Men out of the East were they,
And they traveled by night and they slept
  by day,
 For their guide was a beautiful, wonderful
  star.

The star was so beautiful, large and clear,
 That all the other stars of the sky
Became a white mist in the atmosphere,
And the Wise Men knew that the coming
  was nigh,
 Of the Prince foretold in the prophecy.

Three caskets they bore on their saddle bows,
 Three caskets of gold with golden keys,
Their robes were of crimson silk, with rows
Of bells and pomegranates and furbelows,
 Their turbans like blossoming almond trees.

And so the Three Kings rode into the West,
 Through the dusk of night over hills and
  dells,
And sometimes they nodded with beard on
  breast,

And sometimes they talked, as they paused
    to rest,
With the people they met at the way-side
    wells.

"Of the Child that is born," said Baltazar,
"Good people, I pray you, tell us the news,
For we in the East have seen His star,
And have ridden fast, and have ridden far,
    To find and to worship the King of the
    Jews."

And the people answered, "You ask in vain:
We know of no king but Herod the Great!"
They thought the Wise Men were men insane,
As they spurred their horses across the
    plain,
Like riders in haste who cannot wait.

And when they came to Jerusalem,
    Herod the Great, who had heard this thing,
Sent for the Wise Men and questioned them;
And said: "Go down into Bethlehem,
    And bring me tidings of this new King.

So they rode away; and the star stood still,
    The only one in the grey of morn:
Yes, it stopped; it stood still with its own free
    will,
Right over Bethlehem on the hill,
    The city of David, where Christ was born.

And the Three Kings rode through the gate
    and the guard,
Through the silent street till their horses
    turned
And neighed as they entered the great inn-
    yard;
But the windows were closed and the door was
    barred
    Only a light in the stable burned.

And cradled there in the scented hay,
　In the air made sweet by the breath of kine,
The little Child in the manger lay—
The Child that would be King one day
　Of a kingdom not human but Divine.

His mother, Mary of Nazareth,
　Sat watching beside His place of rest,
Watching the even flow of His breath,
For the joy of life and the terror of death
　Were mingled together in her breast.

They laid their offerings at His feet:
　The gold was their tribute to a King;
The frankincense, with its odor sweet,
Was for the priest the Paraclete,
　The myrrh for the body's burying.

And the mother wondered and bowed her head,
　And sat as still as a statue of stone;
Her heart was troubled, yet comforted,
Remembering what the angel had said
　Of an endless reign and of David's throne.

Then the kings rode out of the city gate,
　With the clatter of hoofs, in proud array,
But they sent not back to Herod the Great,
For they knew his malice and feared his hate,
　And returned to their homes by another way.
　　　　　H. W. Longfellow in *St. Nicholas.*

CHRISTMAS TIME.

HEAP on more wood!—the wind is chill,
But let it whistle as it will,
We 'll keep our Christmas merry still.
Each age has deemed the new-born year
The fittest time for festal cheer:

Even heathen yet, the savage Dane
At Iol more deep the mead did drain;
High on the beach his galleys drew,
And feasted all his pirate crew.

And well our Christian sires of old
Loved when the year its course had rolled,
And brought blithe Christmas back again,
With all his hospitable train.
Domestic and religious rite
Gave honor to the holy night:
On Christmas eve the bells were rung;
On Christmas eve the mass was sung:
That only night, in all the year,
Saw the stoled priest the chalice rear.
The damsel donned her kirtle sheen;
The hall was dressed with holly green:

Forth to the wood did merry men go,
To gather in the mistletoe,
Then opened wide the baron's hall,
To vassal, tenant, serf, and all;
Power laid his rod of rule aside,
And Ceremony doffed his pride.
The heir, with roses in his shoes,
That night might village partner choose;
The lord, underogating, share
The vulgar game of "post and pair."
All hailed, with uncontrolled delight
And general voice, the happy night
That to the cottage, as the crown,
Brought tidings of salvation down.

The fire, with well-dried logs supplied,
Went roaring up the chimney wide;
The huge hall-table's oaken face,
Scrubbed till it shone the day to grace,
Bore then upon its massive board
No mark to part the squire and lord.
Then was brought in the lusty brawn,
By old blue-coated serving-man;

Then the grim boar's head frowned on
    high,
Crusted with bays and rosemary.
Well can the green-garbed ranger tell
How, when and where the monster fell;
What dogs before his death he tore,
And all the baiting of the boar.
The wassail round, in good brown bowls,
Garnished with ribbons blithely trowls.
There the huge sirloin reeked; hard by
Plum-porridge stood, and Christmas pie;
Nor failed old Scotland to produce,
At such high-tide, her savory goose.
Then came the merry maskers in,
And carols roared with blithesome din;
If unmelodious was the song.
It was a hearty note and strong.
Who lists may in their mumming see
Traces of ancient mystery;
White skirts supplied the masquerade,
And smutted cheeks the visors made;
But, O, what maskers richly dight
Can boast of bosoms half so light!
England was merry England, when
Old Christmas brought his sports again.
'Twas Christmas broached the mightiest
    ale;
'Twas Christmas told the merriest tale;
A Christmas gambol oft could cheer
The poor man's heart through half the
    year.
                Sir Walter Scott.

THE CHRISTMAS STORY.

WHILE shepherds watched their flocks by
    night
  All seated on the ground,
The angel of the Lord came down,
  And glory shone around.

"Fear not," said he, for mighty dread
  Had seized their troubled mind;
"Glad tidings of great joy I bring
  To you, and all mankind.

"To you, in David's town, this day
  Is born of David's line,
The Saviour, who is Christ the Lord;
  And this shall be the sign.

"The heavenly Babe you there shall find,
  To human view displayed,
All meanly wrapped in swaddling bands,
  And in a manger laid."

Thus spake the seraph; and forthwith
  Appeared a shining throng
Of angels, praising God, who thus
  Addressed their joyful song:

"All glory be to God on high.
  And to the earth be peace;
Good-will henceforth from heaven to men
  Begin and never cease.
            Nahum Tate.

JACKY'S SOCK AND JENNIE'S STOCKING.

'Twas Christmas eve—and from a chair
  Near which sat mamma softly rocking;
Suspended hung, ill-mated pair,
  Dear Jacky's sock, and Jennie's stocking.

The wee sma' sock, home-made and gray,
  Was suited to the sturdy boot,
Which kept the winter's storms at bay,
  And safely housed the dimpled foot.

The lassie's stocking, fine and new,
  Came o'er the waves from sunny France;
Around the stripes of varied hue
  A prisoned rainbow seemed to dance.

The mother gazes at the twain,
  As she still sits there softly rocking—
A mist of tears, like summer rain,
  Hides Jacky's sock—and Jennie's stocking.

"O Father dear!" she softly prays,
  "My darling children's feet e'er guide,
O lead them through the pleasant ways,
  And keep them ever near thy side!

Another prayer, as fervent quite,
  Was wafted from the little bed,
Where, side by side, that self-same night,
  With folded hands and upraised heads,

The children asked their Dearest Friend,
  (While 'neath their room mamma was rocking),
"Dear Jesus! please Kriss Kringle send,
  To fill up both our sock and stocking."

As if in answer to their prayer,
  Mamma has ceased her steady rocking.
And lo! what curious changes are
  In Jacky's sock—and Jennie's stocking.

From top to toe they're both swelled out
  With queer-shaped bunches, odd and funny,
They surely cannot hold the gout,—
  It must be bon-bons sweet as honey.

The tiny sock, so short and small,
  Is queerly pieced out from the toe,
Below which swings a rubber ball,
  And top that's warranted to go.

Above the leg a whip sticks out—
And wooly dog looks calmly down,
Conjecturing what it's all about,
And whether he should bark or frown.

From out the stocking's top—see! peep
That joyous, beaming little face—
A lovely doll! whose ringlets sweep
Far downward, with unconscious grace.

She's fenced around with little toys,
That glance out brightly here and there—
Gay tokens of the Christmas joys
Which good old Santa Claus doth bear.

The mother sits again to think—
Once more the chair in gently rocking—
The dog and dolly seem to wink
'Cross Jacky's sock and Jennie's stocking.
Helen Stannard.

BRIGHTEST AND BEST.

BRIGHTEST and best of the sons of the morning!
Dawn on our darkness and lend us Thine aid.
Star of the East, the horizon adorning,
Guide where our infant Redeemer is laid!

Cold on His cradle the dew-drops are shining;
Low lies His head with the beasts of the stall;
Angels adore Him in slumber reclining,
Maker and monarch and Saviour of all.

Say, shall we yield Him, in costly devotion,
Odors of Edom and offerings divine?

Gems of the mountain, and pearls of the
  ocean,
Myrrh from the forest, or gold from the
  mine?

Vainly we offer each ample oblation;
  Vainly with gifts would His favor secure;
Richer by far is the heart's adoration;
  Dearer to God are the prayers of the poor.

Brightest and best of the sons of the morning!
  Dawn on our darkness and lend us thine
  aid!
Star of the East the horizon adorning
  Guide where our infant Redeemer is laid!
Reginald Heber.

CONTENTMENT.

"I WISH I had yon golden star,
  I'd wreathe it in my hair;
Look, sister, how it shines afar!
  'Tis like a jewel rare!"

"Yes, love; but see! you might have had
  A treasure far more sweet;
In gazing on that *star*, you've crushed
  The *Heart's-ease* at your feet!"
Frances S. Osgood.

www.ingramcontent.com/pod-product-compliance
Lightning Source LLC
Chambersburg PA
CBHW031814230426
43669CB00009B/1135